Gift from Congregational Church.
Webster Groves, Mo.

12.9.53

Wake Up
or
Blow Up

AMERICA:

Lift the World or Lose It!

by

FRANK C. LAUBACH

Frank C. Laubach

Westwood
FLEMING H. REVELL COMPANY
Los Angeles, London and Glasgow

Copyright, 1951, by

Fleming H. Revell Company

Books by FRANK C. LAUBACH

WAKE UP OR BLOW UP

STREAMLINED ENGLISH LESSONS

MAKING EVERYBODY'S WORLD SAFE

PRAYER, THE MIGHTIEST FORCE IN THE WORLD

THE SILENT BILLION SPEAK

YOU ARE MY FRIENDS

316 Third Ave., Westwood, New Jersey
2173 Colorado Blvd., Los Angeles 41, Calif.
29 Ludgate Hill, London E.C. 4, England
229 Bothwell St., Glasgow C. 2, Scotland

Printed in the United States of America

Contents

CONTENTS

This Book in Brief

A third world war can end in any horror, perhaps even the destruction of the United States. We can prevent that war.

Communism has been winning a cold war since 1920.

We can prevent Communism from taking the rest of the world.

We can do these things the moment we see how and begin to do them.

Bombs and jet planes cannot win cold wars.

The bottom four-fifths of the world are going Communist because they are hungry, terribly unhappy, and grimly determined to rise out of their destitution.

We can stop Communism cold by lifting those wretched people above their misery and desperation. We can do it by sharing our know-how. They love us when we help them; they hate us when we don't.

They are not satisfied with old clothes, surplus food, loans of money. They want to rise to our level. They will settle for nothing less.

They lack progressive methods, and will follow anyone who promises to help them rise.

The Communists, out to capture the world, studied these desires and promised everything.

Our error is that we gave these masses few promises, after Woodrow Wilson first promised and then cracked up; since then little hope has been offered them, and our deeds have been totally inadequate to the vast need.

Where we did help, the results were miraculous. The few technical experts we sent abroad have had tremendous success.

One missionary in every three helps with education and medicine, and a handful of missionaries help with agriculture. Everybody loves them, and treats them like kings. Missionaries clamor for America to contribute this aid on a world scale.

I have worked with missionaries in adult education in sixty-eight countries.

I have worked with the educational departments of fifty governments.

I have mingled with the illiterate three-fifths of the human race, taught them, listened to their pleas, seen their eagerness to learn, their boundless gratitude for a chance to learn, the pathetic way they follow any leader who loves them.

Where we go with literacy, or medicine, or agriculture, they throng to us, love us, follow us, want our religion.

They are as easy to win, if we are there to do it, as a hungry man is to feed.

We could make Christians out of one billion two hundred million illiterate non-Christians if we taught them, helped them better their conditions, and so revealed to them the love of Christ.

No country which I have visited prevents us from carrying out our program of "each one teach and win one." Fifty countries *invite* us to help them.

But there is less than one missionary, Catholic or Protestant, with technical training of any kind, for every 100,000 illiterate non-Christians. Not one missionary trained to write for new literates in two millions! Not one missionary trained in agriculture for every twelve million illiterates.

The United Nations and the United States have adopted a plan to help needy areas with technical aid.

Governments, business, philanthropy, and the Church should unite in an all-out, nation-wide, world-wide attack on world poverty, disease, and oppression by helping people to help themselves.

We could conquer the world's heart by serving it, as Jesus said we should. But in this all-out attack of help, the Church has a very basic responsibility. It must find the right kind of men.

The technicians will fail unless they have the type of character that the Church at its best produces: men with high honor, good habits, integrity, warm heart, Christlike compassionate desire to help—democratic and congenial men who are "color blind," loving, and beloved.

Such men would do as much to raise the ideals of people as they would to teach skills. They would be living witnesses for Christ, and living witnesses for America at her best.

With 100,000 such men strategically planted over the world, our Christian way of life would become popular, and the counsels of violence, revolution, hate, murder, robbery, and lies, would dry up and blow away, because there would be nothing to be violent about. People don't want to murder anybody when they are hopeful and happy and grateful. At least half of those hundred thousand men should be supported by the churches.

Christian missions ought to send out at least 50,000 highly trained technical experts wherever they are wanted. This would cost two billion dollars a year. That money would be available if each church member would set aside five per cent of his income for this foreign-mission program—an average of a dollar a week per member.

We must also appeal to all governments to give every farmer enough land on which to work for himself. There is no good teaching him how to farm if he has no land. Land reform can be effected by purchasing the great feudal estates and reselling to tenants, as was done in Northern Ireland, or by co-operative farming, and by reclaiming hundreds of millions of acres of now dry and useless land.

The Crusade for Freedom and the Voice of America will be mockery until we do this. If we talk about the glory of our freedom, the hungry people, thinking only of food, will ask: "Do you mean freedom from want? What are you doing about it?"

If we start this program on an adequate scale we shall have the desperate, retarded areas of the world back of us within two years, and the threat of this hour will melt like fog before the sun. Our experiences in many countries indicate that it requires from one to two years to change hatred to love, if we do it this way.

This is 100 per cent the way of Christ, who said that anybody in trouble is our neighbor; so help him and love him.

This is the *only* way to convert Russia to the way of Christ.

As surprising world-wide kindness wins the nations, the Communists in Russia will see that violence and hate die out like a candle against loving service, and they will change over to our weapons. Then we shall have a war of kindness to conquer the heart of the world! Who could ask more?

Is this too good to be true? Not unless we are too selfish to try it. Let's try Christianity! It has never been tried by the nations.

But time is running out; it will soon be too late. So be a missionary to everybody you meet; tell him this is the way out. Start your missionaries moving, or go yourself. Pay what every Christian ought to pay. Success depends upon *how many* do their part adequately.

And pray. Pray for the delegates of the United Nations and write and tell them you are praying for them.

Thus you will become powerful in two directions for bringing in the peace.

You have been looking for the answer. *You* are the answer, if you do what every Christian ought to do.

But refusing to be the answer, or even being satisfied with half an answer, is asking for disaster.

If we fail because the majority refuse to help, if we are blown up, we shall be able at least to face the great Judge and hear Him say:

"Well done, good and faithful servant; . . . enter thou into the joy of thy lord."

The way to lay up a treasure in heaven is to help human need. It is the only way that Jesus ever gave us. What we hold we lose, what we use to help others is ours forever.

This résumé is necessarily bare, unsupported assertion; the proof lies in the pages which follow.

If true, this is enormously urgent. It is too urgent to be thrown aside without careful study. Too urgent not to press upon the attention of everybody you know. It may decide the issue of survival.

You will not like all of this book; some of it will sting and hurt you. But when you have finished, you will see a glorious vision, you will know the only answer to our dilemma, and you will see that answer within your grasp, for you will be part of the answer.

For here is the way, the only way to save our country, our world, and our loved ones from being swept over the brink of unthinkable horror.

So let it hurt! Your pain is part of the birth pangs of a new world.

If the book lacks polish, so does hot lava. It was written to try to help save the world, and printed posthaste. It was written to call America's attention sharply to the only issue that matters now: whether America will wake up or blow up!

CHAPTER 1

You Can't Win a Cold War with Hot Weapons

How to Survive an Atomic Bomb is a best seller on nearly every newsstand. It pretends to allay your fears. Death, it assures you, isn't certain—only probable! If you were not blown to smithereens, and if you were not too near to the bomb, and if you hid behind something in three seconds, and if you scrubbed everything hard enough, you might be lucky and survive the first bomb. So why worry?

LET'S TRY CHRISTIANITY

But I do worry. My heart and soul and mind burn to save America and the world from being struck by an atom bomb. Especially am I excited because the true way to peace and survival is precisely the Way of Christ. This book is a lesson in applied Christianity, all of it, though it may sound too practical and self-evident for religion. But Jesus was practical and self-evident, if only people had been wise enough to try Him.

15

It Has Been War for Thirty Years

By now, Americans must see that we have been in
a war for thirty years, a war sometimes hot and sometimes cold, a war of ideas. When the Communists
set out to conquer the world in 1920, they knew it
was war and they fight with every weapon available.
There are no rules, no forbidden holds in their war. If
alliances are useful they make them. If lies are useful
they tell them, if smiles are useful they smile, if talking one way while acting the other is useful, they do
that. There is just one morality and that is to win.

We Americans did not know we were living in a
world at war. We thought we were living in a world
at peace. If we read Communist Manifestos, we did
not take them seriously. Part of Russian strategy was
to keep us thinking it was not war, for this placed us
at a tremendous disadvantage. We were also plagued
by our Christian ideals, and "conscience doth make
cowards of us all." Communists were not embarrassed
by our code of morals.

There is this strange difference between us: for
thirty years the Communists have *known* it was war
to the finish, while we did not know there was a war.
That gave the Communists the tremendous initial
advantage.

The Communists are not the first people who set
out to win the world with ideas. The Christian Church
was like that at the beginning. St. Paul went forth to
conquer the world for the gospel of Christ. The rest
of the world ignored the Christians until they were
so strong that they could no longer be ignored. The

Church for the most part has lost its first passion for conquest. Missionaries alone burned with that early fervor. They knew it was war. The Roman Catholic Church knew that the Communists had declared war. The rest of us thought we were at peace.

The invasion of South Korea at last convinced everybody that this is indeed war. It is a strange war, more like a missionary crusade than a military campaign. How shall we win it? In ordinary wars we always call on the military experts and build up armies and armaments. We are doing that now, to prevent Russia from attempting any more *hot wars* like Korea. But in this queer struggle which we call a cold war military experts are puzzled. They know how to kill soldiers, but in this conflict "we do not war after the flesh." We are bewildered. We are trying to discover what weapons to use.

The purpose of this book is to prove that the missionaries have the answer. We need only wage our war with the weapons Christ provided, and we shall win. These weapons are compassionate service, truth, justice, democratic friendliness. We need have no iron curtain, no secrecy, no hidden weapon. We may openly advertise our weapons to the Communists, for they can neither oppose these weapons nor hate us for using them.

The Communists are able to make little headway among prosperous people. It was among the wretchedly hungry and discontented that the Communists saw their opportunity to conquer the world. So with great cunning they went among these people, studied what they wanted, and offered to give them everything, offered to become their champions against the oppressors.

They promised to liberate the desperately unhappy four-fifths of the human race by using the very method which Jesus Christ rejected, the method of violence, revolution, murder, and terror.

Jesus Christ began as champion of the oppressed and the wretched and died on a cross as their saviour. Compassion for the poor is the very heart of the missionary's gospel.*

So the missionary and the Communist make promises to the same unhappy people. But there is a world of difference between the methods they propose to use in helping these unhappy multitudes. The missionaries seek to change the souls of men who are doing wrong, or at most to stop them by peaceful and legal means. The Communists propose to liquidate all who are in power and to clamp iron bars on the minds of people so that they will fill their stomachs (if they do fill them) at the expense of personal freedom.

There are two ways to get rid of enemies. The way of Jesus is to make them friends by befriending them. (A successful politician and a shrewd businessman employ this method habitually.) The other way is to shoot them—the way of gangsters. There are two ways to get rid of oppressors. One is to persuade them to stop oppression, or to compel them to stop by peaceful, legal means (the Christ method). The other method is to become worse than the oppressor by

* If the reader desires to refresh his memory, let him read: Luke 4:18, 6:20–25, 11:46, 16:19–31, 18:22, and the terrible Matt. 25:31–46.

killing him. The Communists believe that powerful oppressors cannot be unsaddled by love or law, and that the realistic way is to form a conspiracy and destroy them and the government which they control.

Where we missionaries have tried the way of Christ it has worked. We know that it will save the world, if America and the other great powers go all out to put it into practice.

This way of Christ has not been tried by nations, although Mahatma Gandhi moved India in that direction while he lived. The country which first employs Christ's method *all out* (not selfishly or stingily) will conquer the *heart* of the world with love—and there is no other true conquest.

If the Communists adopted the plan described in this book they would win the world, and in doing so they would have such a complete rebirth that they could become Christians in the truest sense of the word. Perhaps they *will* be the first to adopt this method. But I hope and believe that the Western World is more likely to adopt it, because we *profess* it in our Christian religion. We will be unconscious hypocrites, betraying our religion, until we do try it.

Up to the present hour the missionaries have in most of Asia and Africa fought nine-tenths of the war of kindness for the oppressed. They have been hurled back and are now retreating only because they are overwhelmingly outnumbered by the Communist missionaries. America has been making the disastrous mistake of supposing that this way of winning the cold war with Communism was ineffectual, and that only arms and bombs are decisive. While Communists have been using *every* method and winning most of their battles with promises and propaganda, we have been depending upon military power.

WHAT MILITARY PREPARATION CAN AND CANNOT DO

As I write, America is getting geared to spend at least fifty billions a year for an indefinite period to excel Russia in military preparation. We hope that this will deter Russia from initiating a hot war. Perhaps it will. If Russia desired a hot war, the best time for her to have begun it was at the beginning of the Korean invasion. It seems less likely today that she desires a shooting war involving Russian troops than it seemed a few months ago.

But none of this military preparation can prevent Russia from winning the cold war. If we place soldiers all over the world, while she infiltrates every country with missionaries promising to help the people, she will capture the heart of the world. Since the world began, foreign troops were never popular in any country during peace time. If our soldiers were popular in peace time they would cease to become soldiers; they would be missionaries instead.

CAN MILITARY PREPARATIONS SAVE US?

Hanson Baldwin, writing in *The New York Times* about "What Korea Has Taught Us," described all the new weapons, and then gives this painful comment:

The trend of weapon development has been toward less security. The plane and the atom bomb, the tremendous increases in ranges and speeds and power have not made any nation on earth more secure but less so. For the first time in its history the United States, with a three dimensional defense problem, has live frontiers, frontiers of the sea and sky, highly vulnerable to assault. . . .

In the air the long term prospects for the defense overtaking the offense look least bright. . . . Civilian defense is essentially passive defense, yet it implies evacuation, dispersion, decentralization and other measures tremendous in scope and terrible in contemplation. The preparation of defense against air attack today is likely to prove far more costly than the preparation for air attack.

Thus the age-old struggle between offense and defense has come of horrible age; the simple duel between spear and shield has been transferred into duels between complex weapons, systems and whole peoples.

(quoted by permission of *The New York Times*).

That gloomy picture well represents the statement of most military writers. The experts all seem to say that we can go bankrupt paying for armaments, only to find less and less security.

The G.I.'s in Korea discovered another thing—what it means to fight armies reckless of life when they outnumber us ten to one, even with the most modern weapons. Richard Johnson, writing to *The New York Times*, December 9, 1950, from Tokio, says:

The discovery that their superiority in weapons . . . was no guarantee of victory has struck a hard blow at the morale of the United States troops fighting in Korea. With an overwhelming advantage in numbers the lightly armed Chinese Communist forces, under constant air harassment, seized and held the initiative, wrecking the United Nations' offensive and forcing a retreat under trying circumstances. . . .

The troops learned on the Korean battlefront that the best they had in the way of equipment was not enough to halt a foe willing and determined to drive forward, taking any amount of losses to reach his objective. . . .

Several American battalion and regimental commanders have said in Korea that this willingness of the enemy to throw in masses of men regardless of losses has reduced the balance achieved by the G.I.'s superior weapons; . . . the enemy's gigantic reserves of manpower tipped the scales in his favor. "We were forced to fight his kind of war on his terms," one field commander said. "The prospect of meeting this challenge is a grim one," he added. He said that to accept the enemy's challenge on these terms could bog the United Nations forces in an endless and costly campaign from which no decisive results could be achieved.

Never, never before were Americans forced to give from a fifth to four-fifths of their income to build up a defense which threatens to grow steadily more dangerous and impossible. That is a bottomless pit.

But we don't need to put all our eggs in that basket!

Let us, at long last, try Christ's way as totally as we have tried war. Christianity has not failed—*we* have failed to try it in international affairs.

We missionaries *know* that if we tried it all out in the thorough way Americans try other things, it would swiftly save the world. We have had our pilot experiments, we have proved that it works, we know what to do, we know what it will cost.

Let's do it while we still have a world.

This is what I mean. To love our neighbor countries

as ourselves in *deed* and in truth would be real international Christianity. America as a nation never *practiced* the second half of that great commandment: "Love thy neighbor as thyself." No nation has loved its neighbor as itself—the very thought of pretending that we did would make the devil laugh.

Yet the Golden Rule would be insignificant in cost and effort as compared to these insane astronomical costs of armament, and if *thoroughly* practiced, it would make armaments obsolete in twenty years.

It is precisely this that President Truman proposed in his Point IV program, and that the United Nations unanimously ratified in its "technical assistance program." It is beyond all question the most thoroughly Christian plan ever presented by governments in international affairs. The President has said:

"We must not be misled into thinking that our only task is to create defenses against aggression. Our whole purpose in creating a strong defense is to permit us to carry on the great constructive tasks of peace. Behind the shield of a strong defense, we must continue to work to bring about better living conditions in the free nations."

Ambassador Waynick, commenting on this, said:

"The United States is now ready to put into operation, on a world-wide scale, an undertaking of great significance and even greater simplicity. In the midst of global and total diplomacy, complicated by mixed ideologies and confused by a doctrine of deception, the Point IV Program seeks the simple basic thing of helping our neighbors to help themselves. . . ."

Point IV is being launched in a period of emergency, but it is not an emergency program. Rather, it is a long-range effort to help correct some of the fundamental economic and social problems of the world which are among the principal causes of upheaval and war. Point IV is a positive, dynamic movement for creating the basic economic conditions essential for a free, peaceful, and prosperous world society. It would be necessary and desirable even if we were not confronted with a totalitarian conspiracy that masquerades as a new form of democracy with false promises of a better life for all.

Even if you are less sanguine than I am about its results, it would be relatively inexpensive to try it. And if we get blown to heaven, we shall at least be able to face the great Judge and say that we *tried* the Christian way. Today we cannot do that. We are contemptible hypocrites in the eyes of God and man because we try to deceive ourselves and God and man into believing that we are acting as Christians.

It is Christmas day, 1950, as I write. All day on the radio they have been preaching and singing and praying about the Prince of Peace. The Christian world *answers* right, *sings* right at Christmas time— this *do*, America, and thou shalt live! Do it in all international affairs and peace will come almost at once. The tiny army of us who have tried it abroad tingle with the miracle it works. Let's all try it together, unselfishly, and see whether it works on a world scale as it does on a small scale. If it doesn't work, then Christ's plan is futile, as the Communists say it is, and we should stop pretending to believe it.

But it does work. It's the one thing that never fails.

You businessmen know that to get and keep business you must convince people that you are serving them. You politicians know that to win votes you must convince people that you are helping them. You teachers know that to win the love of students you must prove that you love them by your helpfulness. You husbands and wives know that unselfish love alone can make a happy home—each seeking first the joy of the other. You lovers will never win your lady loves until you put this magic into practice. Christian love works wherever it is tried. So try it for the first time on an international scale!

Try it, America, and the world will sing your praises.

Try it, and heaven will sing your praises.

If the smart men in the Kremlin see us succeeding with unselfish service, and if they compete with us in *being helpful,* if we have a war of astonishing kindness—then will the kingdom of heaven be at hand!

This is the game at which we can beat the Politburo. We cannot equal them in lying, or in conspiracy, or in starting revolutions, or in sabotage, or in murder. But we *can* beat them in selling the spirit of Christmas—we have been rehearsing it every year for two thousand years.

It is not *things* that we shall offer to the world. We shall offer our sons, our best beloved sons, send them out to heal the world's wounds, to turn hate into love, sin into virtue, and despair into joy; giving *our* sons as He gave His beloved Son because He so loved the world.

The majority of Christians have forgotten that our

faith started as a flaming crusade to prepare the whole world for the coming of the kingdom of God. Forgetting the flaming crusade, most Christians devote their talents and their time to making money and spending it on comforts for themselves and their families. The so-called "Christian nations" have had a really tremendous crusade—but it was to go forth and exploit the world for profit, *not* to save it. Lured by gold and not by zeal for the kingdom of God, "Christians" have spread all over the world to take all they could get. We did not lift the Asiatics or the Africans to our level. We exploited their poverty for our profit.

This was the great denial and the great betrayal of the Cause of Christ. This is the sin which found us out. Our other sins are sins, but this is *the* sin against the whole earth.

We have another chance to repent, probably our very last. If that repentance were sincere our purses would repent and our aims would repent. We would devote our time and strength and money to helping Christ's kingdom to come, and all men everywhere to have "life more abundantly."

If we do repent in 1951 and put the mighty shoulder of America under the world to lift and heal its wounds and wipe away its tears, and if we do that without taint of greed, we shall conquer the world's heart in two years. Before that weapon Russian communists will be helpless. Indeed, Russia will be compelled to fall in behind that crusade.

When President Truman proposed that idea in his Point IV, every nation on earth, *including Russia and her satellites,* endorsed it without a single word of opposition. It was too popular; no nation dared to oppose it.

One man caught his breath when he realized the stupendous somersault in our life habits that this plan would involve, and asked, "Do you imagine America could be persuaded to do anything as revolutionary as this? That would be a miracle—nothing less than a new birth."

I replied, "Such miracles happen when men get in foxholes. And we are in a foxhole."

Chapter 2

The World's Hungry

Businessmen are always on the alert for opportunities. I will try to talk their language. The most stupendous opportunity to meet a felt need began just after the first World War, and it gets bigger and better every year. It is new and it includes four-fifths of the world.

This opportunity is due to the titanic efforts of the hungry, destitute masses of Asia, Africa, Latin America, and Europe to escape from their misery. They were in despair, but now they are making up their minds that they will come up—or blow up the world. They are desperate, grim, irresistible.

Our opportunity is to help them up. Our doom is to seem to block their path.

That is the new stupendous crisis, involving four-fifths of the world.

That rising tide is so awful that all other things that go with that tide will also rise, or be deluged if they try to go against it. This is true of the United Nations, democracy, Communism, education, industry, the press and all armies. Edwin Markham said that the dumb thing will speak after the silence of the centuries; it is speaking now, and what it says is this: "I am coming up, and I will take the hand of anybody who helps me up, and destroy any man who is in my way."

I had nothing to do with starting this world upheaval. I did not encourage it—but I *saw* it. Anybody but a blind man would see it if he worked among these masses in more than seventy countries, as I have done.

Age-old Want

Poverty and famine and misery are not new. They have always existed, as terrible as they are today and often worse. Man's inhumanity to man shrieks so loudly that it is hard to understand how God can stand the human race. The world has always been driven by severe and, often, cruel masters. There is nothing new about that.

But the multitudes submitted and suffered and died in sad and sullen despair. Their religions told them that poverty was fate, kismet, and that they would be set free only after they died.

The New Grim Determination

But this new thing that took birth after the first World War is not sullen despair. It is sullen, but it is not despair; it is grim purpose to come up out of misery. It is not for nothing that four-fifths of the human race have changed from a state of despair to a new grim resolve to come up from poverty and oppression; that determination is growing everywhere and growing with ever-accelerating rapidity. In some countries, like the United States, Australia and England, the laborers have banded together in labor unions and have been able to free themselves from poverty. People who live in these countries are likely to be blind to the misery and to the desperate state of mind of the masses in the rest of the world. Unless the reader of these pages has lived among them he will find here a startling and terrifying revelation of something commentators seldom mention, because they, too, are ignorant of it. Yet it is the most colossal and ominous fact in the world, and the most wonderful fact, for any nation that is prepared to help the suppressed masses realize their hope.

Let us get clearly in mind how many people we are talking about, and where they are. Out of the 2200 million people in the world, 1700 million, usually in debt all of their lives, are in want, more or less oppressed and exploited, and increasingly unhappy and determined to be free from want. They are not in the United States, except a million or two migrant workers and many of the Negroes; they are not in Canada, the United Kingdom, or in the Scandinavian countries. But in all the rest of the world there are multitudes dissatisfied and groping for some way up and out of the dark drudgery and pain of empty living.

THE CHANGE FROM DESPAIR TO
DESPERATE DETERMINATION

What caused this tremendous change from sullen hopelessness to grim resolve? A great many factors.

The first were the teachings of Jesus, especially the gospel of Luke and the companion Book of Acts. Here was "good news for the poor, release to the captives, liberty to those who are oppressed, sight to the blind. . . . Today," declared Jesus, "this scripture has been fulfilled in your hearing" (Luke 4:18-21). "Blessed are you poor, blessed are you that hunger now, for you shall be satisfied; blessed are you that weep now, for you shall laugh. Woe to you that are rich, woe to you that are full now, for you shall hunger" (Luke 6:20-25). These words are so terrible that few preachers dare read them from the pulpit. The words, the compassionate deeds of Christ, and His death made Him the friend of the poor, of sinners, of outcasts. It is very likely that the millions who zealously distributed the Bible never realized what new hope and what strong new determination the poor and oppressed derived from Jesus. Perhaps we can interpret His words as meaning "pie in the sky by-and-by" but the people who heard Him thought He meant a "kingdom of God *here*," and He did! "Thy kingdom come . . . in earth, as it is in heaven" cannot be twisted to mean anything but what it says. That prayer is more often repeated than any other in history. It included "our daily bread" and forgiveness of debts and deliverance from evil. It stirred and still stirs up infinite longings where people felt only infinite despair. Many of the Old Testament prophets were just as zealous for social righteousness as was Jesus. For all these years missionaries have been spreading this gospel of hope, and even though they were not stirrers up of the people, the Bible was. The Bible is dynamite, and it is the most widely sold book of all time.

But the thing which has really broken the masses loose from their moorings in the retarded areas is the vast new network of communications. The Portuguese, Italian, Dutch, French, and English explorers of the fifteenth to the eighteenth centuries started it. Then came steamships, railways, automobiles, trucks, and good roads and autobuses (which are now incalculably important all over the world); then airplanes, motion pictures and telephones, businessmen in swank homes, countless business enterprises, with radios and the sewing machine always out in front; then World War I, with our soldiers going everywhere, well fed, generous with their money; then tourists sweeping by—all these factors together produced in the hungry masses a great envy and a great longing to be like these "millionaires," a great longing to better the condition of their children, to rise out of their wretched hovels to the new level that they saw in these foreigners. This turn took a sudden rise in 1920 and it has been rising ever since, with ever-greater momentum.

Not the least of the causes of this new determination were the beautiful promises of Woodrow Wilson at the end of the first World War. No words in all history have so electrified the world. When Wilson went to Europe to build the League of Nations, his beautiful dream was being repeated in every corner of the world. No man before or since has aroused such passionate longings. Had Wilson not been opposed by little selfish men as he sought to give justice to Eu-

rope and as he tried to sell his League of Nations to
America, we probably would never have had World
War II. But the world was not yet ready for his stupendous vision. Perhaps, too, Wilson helped defeat
himself. At all events, the world lost its great incredible hope. Now it has its second chance in the United
Nations.

One must also recognize the enormous influence
which Mahatma Gandhi wielded upon India and the
entire world. Capturing the true revolutionary spirit
of Jesus from his reading of the New Testament, Gandhi forged his program of non-violent and loving
non-co-operation, and he won the freedom of India
without firing a gun. Won it loving those who opposed it! In China, Sun Yat Sen had already per-
formed an equally prodigious service by breaking
from ancient imperialism and embracing the new
ideals of democracy.

It was at this time that Communism came upon the
scene in Russia, adopting the philosophy and program of Marxian Socialism. When the Communists
set out to conquer the earth, they at once saw their
opportunity in this stupendous new determination of
the hungry majority of the world to come up out of
their misery. The Communists saw that they could
not win over the people who were satisfied; it was
therefore among the discontented that they began
their clever propaganda, discovering their grievances,
fanning them into a hotter flame, and promising anything that the people wanted. The Russian Communists were seasoned masters of this type of intrigue
and propaganda, for they had worked underground

to overthrow the Czarist regime for many years. Josef Stalin was one of the cleverest of all the underground workers.

Stalin and the Politburo have proven themselves to be keen analysts of the world situation and amazingly clever in promising what the discontented people want. Because socialism is not what the disinherited wanted; they gave up socialism and adopted exactly the opposite, *private ownership of the land*. Because Sun Yat Sen and multitudes of others had preached democracy, they thought they had "freedom" and "democracy," although it is in reality the opposite—it is despotism. But the hungry people of the world are illiterate and they can easily be deceived. Like Esau, the masses will sell freedom for the promise of a full stomach. After the Iron Curtain falls it is too late, for he who protests disappears.

It is amazing that we have allowed Russia to offer these two most attractive qualities of American life, private ownership of land and individual freedom, although she plans ultimately to take away both land and freedom. We have allowed the Russians to outsmart us.

They have jostled us into co-operating with imperialistic powers until in several notorious instances we are backing oppression, the very thing America hates. For example, in French Indo-China most Asiatics want France to leave; yet we have loaned France over three billion dollars, knowing that the money is being used to suppress all opposition to the French in Indo-China.

Chess is now the great Russian game, encouraged

and subsidized by the government. Russian leaders believe that chess develops mental acumen. The men in the Kremlin are playing an exceedingly clever chess game for the domination of the world. Icy cool, unemotional, without sentiment, they deliberate before they call the plays, and thus far we have walked into their traps.

It is time for us to take the initiative and call the plays! America could do that with an all-out drive to help the hungry people of the world out of their misery, finding out what they need and giving it to them and asking nothing in return. That would be doing what the Communists promise to do. The weapon of selfless kindness need not be concealed. The clearer it is seen by the world, the more invincible it becomes!

Why has America not gone all-out for this kind of service before? It is anybody's guess. Most of us have been enormously obsessed with America. Many have thought of the rest of the world only in terms of trade. Only a small part of the people of this country have been actively engaged in foreign missions. Indeed, only a very small proportion of our American Christians have had any interest at all in foreign missions.

Russia is trying frantically to keep us split from China, and that is one excellent reason why we should refuse to be split from China! We need China, and China needs us. We have been her friend, more consistently than any other country. When she adopted Communist revolutionary methods to get a redeal in land, she adopted *the American land system, and not socialism.*

When I said this in a western college, a Chinese professor stood up and said, "This man knows the truth. The Chinese peasants are not going Communist, for they do not know what Communism is. All they know is that they are hungry and that the Communists promise to give them land and to fill their stomachs. They are not Communists; they are come-up-ists."

As I write today the American representative in the United Nations, Ambassador Warren Austin, is protesting our friendship for China, and he is mentioning our contribution in schools and hospitals and in other forms of missionary service in China. How we wish that contribution were a hundred times greater!

This book is written to urge all America to join in unselfish, lavish, loving service; with that we would have something to boast about! That, if we are sincere and all-out, would start such a wave of love for America across the world that nobody would listen to those who call us indifferent, or exploiters, or selfish. We have a tremendous advantage over the Kremlin in that we *believe* in the private ownership they now offer temporarily because they must offer it. We *believe* in the way of unselfish service, because that is the way of Christ.

I am interested not only in making this case clear to America. I am praying that it may make every American an enthusiastic missionary, burning to back this plan for lifting the world out of its dangerous and horrible misery. Then and then only will our Christianity be honest Christianity. Then and then only will it be adequate.

CHAPTER 3

Missions Retreated and the Communists Walked In

It was the irony of history that just as this tremendous new determination of the retarded peoples to rise out of poverty to our level began to develop, the Christian Church began to lose her enthusiasm for missions. She became "broad-minded." Unfortunately, I cannot here discuss all the causes of this coolness toward missions and shall mention only one. It is the utterly false description of idyllic primitive conditions by professors of anthropology and sociology who never crossed an ocean nor visited a Negro slum, but who describe those who live there as happy, better off indeed than we are. Here is a letter from a woman steeped in this soothing falsehood:

> Los Angeles, California
> July 11th, 1949

Dear Dr. Laubach:

After hearing your talk at Bethany Presbyterian Church yesterday, I am inspired to write this letter. It is written in a spirit of love, and of appreciation of that part of your work which looks to me morally legitimate and good. Please consider your possible mistakes as follows:

You are taking to primitive peoples Bread, in the form of Literacy which is tied in with concealed poison in the shape of an alien culture.

Note the stage of evolution of the remote people of New Guinea. According to your own words, they are naked, polygamous cannibals. Well, in certain climates, and for such people, there is nothing undesirable or immoral about nudity. Why seek to rob them of their naturalness, and complicate their lives with *body* consciousness and clothes?

Polygamy may be best for some Races in some stages of development. Any attempt to thrust a different culture upon such people may only cause confusion, psychological maladjustment, and dislocations in their social order.

And what about cannibalism? Is the eating of human flesh any worse than killing and eating our defenseless little Brother, the Cow and the Sheep? Is cannibalism any worse than vivisection as practised by our Scientists? Is it any worse than the greed and warmongering of our Western "Civilized Culture"? I believe that bullfighting and prize fighting are more degrading than cannibalism.

Religion is natural and good; that is, Religion that is indigenous to the (Social) soil of a People. Jesus' teaching is universal, and no doubt is the highest yet brought forth on this Planet. But Christianity and its fantastic theology is only a Western distortion of the exalted teachings of the gentle Oriental, Jesus of Nazareth. Paul's theology began the distortions. And the Church has mostly followed Paul and not Jesus. But anyway, the highest and purest concepts of the way of Life that Jesus gave to the world we should seek to *incorporate* into native Religions, not try to thrust Christianity onto peoples as a substitute for their own concepts and traditions. It is shocking and bad that the Japanese should forsake their own gods for other peoples' gods, as in their wholesale adoption of Christianity, which you mentioned.

Why waste time and energy combating anything so sane and good as Communism? It is not good for this country but it may be good for some people. If the Communists are Atheists, that is not too bad, so long as they teach and practice Human Brotherhood, and the way of life that Jesus taught. Consider the harm that you may be doing, the trouble you may be fomenting by combating the teachings and work of the Communists in the Orient. The crimes of a Power Culture and of Capitalistic exploitation of human beings are the worst on Earth. And a Religion (that is Christianity) which is unescapably tied in with Power Politics, and Commercial exploitation of primitive peoples cannot but harm them more than it benefits them.

You have much to give that is good, if you will only separate it from the mistake of interfering with the spread of Communism, and if you will avoid dislocating native cultures.

The fact that many primitive peoples seek eagerly for what you have to give does not justify your tricking them into adopting Christianity along with their acquisition of a written language. Your campaign for literacy is a wonderful enterprise, but why vitiate it with the mistakes of our Christianity, and of our Western culture?

Sincerely,

B—— H——

It was teaching like this in our colleges and schools (among other things) that undermined our interest in missions. So the missionaries in some leading denominations have actually diminished in numbers while their resources diminished in real value by the decline of the dollar.

That the interest of American church members in missions has not risen at all in these thirty years of cold war is shown by these astonishing statistics. Charles Fahs of the Missionary Research Library discovered that the per capita giving from living donors for foreign missions in 1920 for eleven leading denominations in the United States was $1.66.[*]

The same eleven denominations, according to the United Stewardship Council's statistics of December, 1949, showed a per capita giving for foreign missions of $1.15 (as compared to $1.66 in 1920), or a decrease in per capita giving of 51 cents, in those 29 years.

The number of missionaries for these eleven denominations has decreased from 5,373 in 1919 to 4,587 in 1948, or a decrease of 786.[**]

Another way of estimating how missionary giving has gone down is to study the published statistics of foreign missionary *expenditures* since 1928, in mission boards. Those statistics show that for some 120 boards, a total of 32 million dollars was expended in 1928-1930; by 1934 it had dropped steadily to 21 million dollars; in 1942 it had reached a low of 16 million, and then it started to rise again. In 1944 it was 20 million, in 1946 it was 31 million, and by 1947 it was up to 35 million—three million above the figure

[*] *Trends in Protestant Giving*, 1929, p. 53.

[**] This corresponds with another report of the Foreign Missions Conference from fifteen denominations, which shows that they had 6,087 missionaries in 1919, and 5,192 missionaries in 1948. (*World Almanac*, 1949, p. 433).

for 1928. Thus, there is a seeming rise or increase back to 1947, but that is an illusion, inasmuch as goods that cost $1.22 in 1928 would cost $1.59 in 1947. That means that 35 million dollars in 1947 is the equivalent of only 27 million dollars in 1928. So there was a real loss of 8 million dollars between 1928 and 1947. The decreased interest in missions is even more apparent when we compare *giving* and *incomes*.

Look at this: in 1929 the per capita income in our country was $680. *In 1947 the per capita income was $1,323.* Almost double! But the total expenditures for foreign missions, as we saw above, increased only ten per cent, while per capita giving went down.

The United Stewardship Council says that the average American Protestant member's giving for foreign missions in 1949 was $1.25. The average income in the U.S.A. in 1949 was $1,453. The average church member therefore gave, to win the cold war through missions, 9/100 of 1% of his income. He was *compelled* to give 25% to 75% of his income for military preparations. This means that while the *average* church member gives less than ½ a cent a day for foreign missions, he gives more than $1.50 a day for war.

Yet a few days ago a man told me that we might as well pull all our missionaries out, inasmuch as they are so ineffectual against the Communists! I replied, "Do you ever give anything for foreign missions?" He replied proudly, "Never." "Better pull the missionaries out" if they can't get along on *nothing!* Does that spirit deserve to survive?

Briefly, so far as three-fourths of the church mem-

bers are concerned, our giving for foreign missions
has been a stupendous fraud. Can we awake soon
enough? I personally think that the survival of the
United States depends upon that more than upon
any other single factor. Thank God for the one-fourth
who have seen the vision and for the one-hundredth
who have tithed for missions!

All in all, American Christians thought it was "missions as usual" and "business as usual." The American
Church did not realize that an enormous world upheaval had taken place, which presented the Christian Church with such a chance as it has not seen in
two thousand years. She was blind, at the moment
when she was confronted with the most marvelous
break-through since Christ walked the earth.

The Communist International, on the other hand,
looking for a way to create a world revolution, saw exactly the break-through they desired in this tremendous urge of four-fifths of the human race to better
their condition. While the Church grew cold to her
own gospel, the Communists sent their missionaries
to convert the natives of every country to their violent
gospel.

The Communist gospel is simple enough to make
its lies sound plausible. It is passed on to the masses
not by foreigners, but by natives converted to
Communism. This is what they preach: "You are
hungry, in debt, without land, oppressed by the landowner. The moneylender and white foreigner and the
government all rob you. That is why you are destitute. Ninety per cent of the people like you are destitute. We will help you start a people's revolution. We

will furnish you with arms; all of us will be armed secretly, then we will make a tremendous attack and overwhelm the government and establish a soviet government of the poor people. We will drive out the rich landowners and the foreigners and divide the land into small farms so that every man can have enough to live in comfort and happiness."

That formula sounds good to the hungry man, for he has long hated the moneylenders and the landowners, especially the foreign landowners. It is a formula of hate, robbery, violence, and murder, but he will follow this course rather than remain in hunger and misery. He is ignorant and not bothered by the laws of property rights.

The hungrier people get, the less binding the rights of others appear. The first right is to survive, so the hungry man believes, at whatever cost. Those who went through the various stages of hunger in the internment camps of the last war testify that they reached a stage where they could think of nothing but food, and finally where nature drove them to steal it. Masses who are close to the hunger line or over it all of the time have no deeply ingrained ethical code to restrain them from stealing or deceit or violence or murder.

For that matter, nearly all of us justify violence when it is called war. It is wrong to murder, but it isn't considered murder if we kill enemies in war; *that* is a victory for the right! So when war has been declared on the government and the landlords, and the moneylenders, the tenants can be persuaded that killing the enemy is victory for the right!

The Communists have presented to the hungry and oppressed multitudes the idea that they are in a righteous war of liberation from their enemies, and this sounds true to oppressed people—a fact that America must understand.

Here is the chief reason why China fell before the Communist propaganda with such amazing speed. The Communists promised a new deal in land, and kept their promise, while the Nationalist government was supported by the rich landowners and so could not make a redistribution. It is also the reason why the people of North Korea fought with such fanatical desperation even when they faced defeat. They had seen the Communists throw out the landlords and divide the land into small plots for the little farmers, and this was enough to prove that Communism was a friend of the masses.

Lest anybody suppose I am a Communist, let me say here that I regard Communism as the most dreadful menace that ever faced the human race. Communism is a stupendous fraud. Its ultimate purpose is not the redistribution of land into small parcels, not freedom, but the confiscation of all land by government, and making all farmers tenants and all men slaves. They get rid of the landlords but they plan to make the state the superlandlord. This the little people do not know, for they never read Marxist doctrine; they know nothing about Communism; they know only that the Communists promise exactly what the people want and that *at first* they keep that promise.

I have wondered why some of our American magazines do not send journalists to find out exactly what the Communists publish that so quickly and easily captures the loyalty of the underprivileged of the earth. These journalists would return, after such an inquiry, with the *one and only* countermove to save these multitudes from going Communist. Indeed, if the statement which I have tried to make simply and clearly is accepted as fact, the reader sees that answer now. It is self-evident.

It is simply to go out and help those people, not on a small scale but on a truly adequate scale, to give them the true American way and not a little taste of it. It is not enough to say, "The Communists are lying. Be content with your poverty." Those masses will never again be content with their poverty. Nothing can stop their upward movement now. Nor will it save us merely to threaten to blow these hungry people to pieces if they dare to raise their heads against their oppressors.

We and the governments which are friendly to us are trying hard to develop a United Nations police force to prevent invasion of any one country by another. That is a sound plan, and perhaps it is the most helpful thing we are doing. And yet the danger we face is that the United Nations will be tempted to use that police force to repress the masses when they rise in agony against their oppressors. That is exactly what some people in the U.N. countries are urging us to do. For example, as I write today, the French delegate in the United Nations is trying to persuade the Assembly to go to France's aid in French Indo-China, as we went to the aid of South Korea, although nearly all of the people of Indo-China and most of the people of Asia want France to leave Indo-China.

If we are to help these people up above the danger line of desperation and hate, if we are to capture their confidence and loyalty, we have two tasks to perform:

1. To help them get out of debt and to get enough land so that every man can till his own soil "the American way," as President Truman has put it.

2. To help them get the technical knowledge of agriculture and its related industries, so that they can use their resources most productively and profitably.

As I write, newspapers and magazines are saying that we must strive for "a clearer understanding of the Asian psychology" (Hanson Baldwin, *New York Times,* Oct. 31, 1950). There is nothing mysterious or difficult about the fundamental fact; it is *the gnawings of hunger and the misery of destitution.* It isn't Asian psychology; it is human psychology—yours and mine. These people have been in despair in the past, but they are becoming more and more like us, determined not to be hungry, not to be oppressed!

This is no mystery to the missionaries. It is as clear as any fact in the world.

What missionaries cannot understand is the attitude of those among us who think it peculiar that some people want their stomachs filled, that they want to be like us, and that they believe the promises of a country which offers to help them, even though it is lying.

When they were shouting "Hosanna" around Jesus during the triumphal march to Jerusalem, He came riding over the brow of the hill and, to the consternation of the multitude, burst into tears over Jerusalem as He moaned:

"Would that today you knew the things that make for peace. But now they are hid from your eyes. The days will come upon you, when your enemies will cast up a bank about you and surround you, and hem you in on every side, and dash you to the ground, you and your children within you, and they will not leave one stone upon another in you, because you did not know the time of your visitation."

It all came true as He foretold, because they put their trust in war and not in His way.

Do you think He is weeping over America today, saying the same words for the same reason? And does it make you weep?

The Church lost faith in the last command of Jesus, "Go ye into all the world," when it lost interest in helping the world to catch up with us; and the Communists, out to capture the world, found it easy. We retreated and they walked in.

It is not too late, *if we wake up*. And we will either wake up or blow up!

Chapter 4

The Greatest Break-Through in History

In the October 28, 1950, issue of the *Saturday Evening Post* appeared this editorial:

> It would seem sensible before getting steamed up too much in this war for men's minds to get some really useful information about what the minds of peasants in Asia are like. One source would certainly be the Christian missionaries. They live and labor among poor people and their testimony ought to be worth at least as much as that of some of the experts.

That is indeed sensible. If we had realized that missionaries were the only Americans we had who lived close to the unhappy masses and knew what they wanted, and if we had supported the missionaries and listened to their advice, we would not be losing the cold war for the world.

Soon after the first World War missionaries began to experience in their own communities this tremendous new urge to come up. Where they used medicine and schools, they found in this service an effective means to melt away prejudice and to win friends for themselves and Jesus Christ.

Most Christian missionaries have been strong for the establishment of elementary schools; they wanted their members to be able to read the Bible or prayer books or hymnbooks. Sometimes these schools were popular and sometimes they were not. In the past thirty years, however, all this has been changed. The world has gone education mad. Thousands of schools began to overflow, and more new schools were needed than the missions could afford to open. Thousands of schools were opened by natives on a self-supporting basis when the missionaries had no funds for them.

But adults were not satisfied just to educate their children. They began to want to learn to read and write themselves. They saw that one reason they were hungry and sick, in rags and hovels, in debt, oppressed and swindled by moneylenders was because they were ignorant. They noticed that the people who had the wealth were literate and that the impoverished people were illiterate. Hitherto they had always longed to read, but to them illiteracy was like poverty—a prison from which they could never escape. They thought schools were for children.

It was during the first World War that all this began to change. The first evidence of the change was among the Chinese coolies in the trenches of France. They had been brought over to dig trenches. Being illiterate, they could neither read letters from China nor write back to their families. James Yen, a Chinese Y.M.C.A. secretary for the coolies in France, wrote so many letters for these homesick Chinese that his fingers hurt. Then he got the idea of teaching them to write their own letters. He chose a thousand Chinese words which would be necessary to write simple letters and taught the coolies how to write their own letters home. The experiment was a great success.

At the end of the World War, Yen returned to China with the coolies, and began to teach people to read his thousand-character vocabulary, again with great success. He had made a stupendous discovery; he had experienced the great new passion of the adult masses to come up through education out of poverty and despair. When people want a thing badly enough it is easy to organize them, and James Yen found here a marvelous easy break-through for service. His campaign spread like wildfire, spread beyond teaching, reading and writing to the other basic needs of people in deep poverty and disease and dirt. The government of China took up this popular cause in one province after another, and Yen believes that fifty million Chinese have learned to read.

Almost simultaneously a second immense advance in literacy began in Russia. Lenin said that Russia could not be united nor made Communist if only twenty per cent of the people could read. So the Communists started a vast compulsory literacy program, adopted a perfect alphabet, taught by the syllabic method, allowed people to study in fifty languages, set a time after which they must read to get a job, required millions to teach without pay—and they report having taught upwards of 100 millions, raising the literacy from twenty per cent to ninety per cent plus.

Meanwhile some fifty mission centers of the world began to sense this new hunger of adults for education, and had interesting though unnoticed local successes. They began to correspond with one another about this interesting new hunger, and to ask the best way of meeting it. The traditional word story method of teaching, now employed in English with children, was proving to be too difficult. The memory load when one must remember how to pronounce each word is too heavy for adults.

Many missionaries, however, dared to be original. Ninety per cent of the languages of the world are almost perfectly phonetic, one sound for a letter. English, on the other hand, is the worst spelled language in the world. We have eight sounds on an average for each of the vowels, and in any new word are not sure which of these eight sounds to give it. "Ough" is pronounced six ways in English. The large English dictionaries have a thousand words few of us can pronounce. But in Spanish you can pronounce any unknown word after from a few days' to a few weeks' study, because there is but one sound for each vowel and consonant. All the languages of India, Africa, and Latin America, all the languages of the Pacific, are perfectly phonetic.

This is why the missionaries who tried teaching syllables had remarkable results. They did not teach the alphabet "abcdefghijklmnopqrstuvwxyz," but when they taught *a, ba, da, fa, ga, ha, ja,* and all the other syllables, in a few days their students could pronounce *any* word without the teacher's help.

Most missionaries are unafraid to try new things. They would not be missionaries if they followed the crowd. They are compelled to be self-reliant and to pioneer. There is a far greater percentage of these fearless experimenters among missionaries than among the people who remain at home. It is not that they are brighter than other people; they are only bolder.

These bold experimenters found that the easier their methods became, the more illiterate adults clamored to learn to read. I was one among hundreds of experimenters. We corresponded with one another, sharing our new, better ideas, growing more and more excited at the results we were getting, the triumphant smiles and the gratitude of our students, the rapidly mounting number of new literates, the thousands of new friends we were making and the numbers who became Christians. Something tremendous was happening.

I happen to be a missionary whose business it is to visit these miracle workers in sixty-eight countries. I have seen the triumph in their eyes, the look of discoverers of a new world, and I have seen a new way to conquer the world for Christ. There are only a few hundred of these educational missionaries who have entered this open door of teaching and winning the illiterate non-Christian world, but they are like me, fanatically sure that down this road of Christian service and witness lies the conquest of the world for Christ. The "riddle of Asia and Africa," which has baffled everybody except the Communists, looks not only soluble but will be *easy* if you will give missions the re-enforcements and the resources they need. A few hundred of us missionaries believe we know how to evangelize and to conquer the world for Christ in this generation, and that this crisis stirred up by the Communists can be made to help Christ. For one thing, the Communists are helping shake conceited, complacent, self-centered America out of her hypnotic stupor.

We are not afraid. God is standing in this new open door and is ringing out that old terrible world we have had and ringing in the new.

We must move and move rapidly, *now*.

CHAPTER 5

How My Eyes Were Opened by the Moros

I should like to tell a little of the experience which has driven so deep into my soul the conviction that down this road lies the way to save the freedom and peace of the world.

While working in Mindanao, Philippines, among the Moslem Moros, we found that they needed only sixteen letters for their sixteen sounds; after a few months of experimentation we learned to teach the Moros all their syllables in a matter of two or three days. We found three key words which contained all the twelve Moro consonant sounds:

ma la ba nga	(name of a Moro town)
ka ra ta sa	("paper" in Moro)
pa ga na da	("to study" or "learn" in Moro)

There were only four vowels in their language: *a, i, o, u.* By mixing these with the consonants, we could write everything and read everything in the Moro language.

When the Moros realized that it was very easy, they came to learn by the dozens, then by the hundreds, and finally by the thousands.

Before we taught the Moros to read, none of them would come to our church. After a few months of the literacy campaign many came, and the younger men who knew English began to join our church. In two years the entire tribe of Moros, hostile when we first arrived, became our warm friends.

We began to correspond with missionaries in other mission countries, Asia, Africa, Latin America, the Pacific Islands, telling our results and asking for their experiences. The answers came back full of fervor, many of them were tingling with local successes like those which we were having, and all of them were eager for help.

At that time I read a book by Daniel Fleming, called *The Marks of a World Christian,* which said that two-thirds of the population of the world could not read, and that ninety per cent of the non-Christian world was illiterate. When I told my Moro friends, "We have found a way to learn that will help two-thirds of the world," they became noisily excited. I was as excited as they. It is a fervor that has not died down in twenty years. We and other missionaries had struck it rich—if helping people and winning friends is what you are seeking.

The literacy campaign of the Moros got the rest of the Philippines excited. At the request of the National Christian Council and with the co-operation of the Department of Education and the Governor General, I helped make similar lessons in about twenty Philippine dialects. All of them were as simple and easy to learn as our lessons for the Moros. All of them were Malay languages, as easy as those in Mindanao—

twelve to fourteen consonants, four vowels, and every syllable ending in a vowel!

In 1935 we returned to America for our furlough, going by way of Asia and the Mediterranean instead of crossing the Pacific. Missionaries, eager to exchange experiences, arranged for our entertainment and for conferences. We tried making lessons in the Malay languages of Singapore and Sumatra. They worked! We tried making lessons in five languages of India, in Arabic at Cairo, Jerusalem and Beirut, and in Turkish at Istanbul. These languages proved much harder than the Malay languages had been, and our first lessons were not very good, but they were an improvement on previous lessons. The enthusiasm of the missionaries and of the illiterates was even greater than we had expected to find. We told a group of New York businessmen about this encouraging experience, and they formed the "World Literacy Committee." I have been traveling as the representative of that Committee for the past fifteen years.

All of these tours have been in co-operation with missions, and in fifty countries in co-operation with governmental departments of education. The visits, lasting from a week to two months in each area, were occupied with conferences with competent linguists and educators.

In each conference we prepared literacy primers (mimeographed copies) and tried them on as many illiterates as we could in the time at our disposal. Then we organized the churches, schools, and other organizations into "each one teach one" campaigns.

I have sat down beside thousands of illiterates and

helped them begin to read. I have seen their response over nearly all the illiterate areas of the world.

The basic conviction expressed in this book was not therefore the result of imagination, but of experiences piling up higher and higher to verify one another in every country. Anybody who had gone through the same experiences would come out with the same certainty that I have, that those who cannot read have a strange, pathetic, even terrible longing to learn to read, when they find it is possible, because they believe that through this door they can get out of their misery.

I did not know this in 1915 when I went to Mindanao as an educational missionary. I had secured my Doctor of Philosophy degree in Sociology and was familiar with the literature of sociologists and anthropologists, who often write poetry about the idyllic happiness of the primitive peoples. But my experience with the illiterate millions all over the world has long since exploded this academic fanatasy. I have found the illiterate people close to the poverty line, seldom able to get all they want to eat, obsessed with the never-ending problem of satisfying their hunger, sick and plagued with flies and vermin and insects and germs which make every day a battle for life. In my generation, at least, the *real* illiterates are just plain unhappy, and I believe this is the true picture of ninety-five per cent of them, from Adam down to today. They were formerly in dismal despair. The new thing about them is that they no longer despair. They now hope; they are like men trapped in a mine desperately struggling to get out.

For many years I have traveled among these people in every continent, and I have seen this new desperate hope rising steadily every year. If it were true only in one country or in a few countries it would still be significant, but I find it true in *every* country.

Educated people differ widely in their attitude toward these new aspirations of the masses, just as people have differed in their attitude toward labor unions in America. Missionaries and some other educated people ardently desire to help the illiterates, but many other people are doubtful, some neutral, some fearful, some hostile. Many see a terrible danger in this yearning of the masses to rise. They had better be afraid to oppose the masses, because this rising tide is certain to destroy any man or any group that stands in its way. This tide is as irresistible as the revolving of the earth.

There are people who for selfish gain seek to keep these people illiterate. In Johannesburg, South Africa, some friends arranged for me to meet the men responsible for securing laborers for the gold mines. The companies, by offering relatively good wages, have lured hundreds of thousands of Negroes from their villages, leaving the wives and children at home. A true picture of the tragic moral conditions of these camps is found in *Cry, the Beloved Country*. I told these gold-mine officials that the camps afforded a fine opportunity to send the men back home with a little education and Christian ideals, so that they in turn could teach the people in their villages; and added that this separation might turn into a blessing to them at least in this respect. The chief official at the table replied:

"We are here on business and we must be practical. Can you show us that if we teach these men to read they will not leave the mines and get better jobs in Johannesburg? Nobody is going to work in a hole a mile deep if he can get out of it. I admit that the ethics are on your side, but we have to mine gold and make it pay."

They have not yet begun a literacy campaign in those gold mines.

On a railroad platform in Kenya Colony I fell to talking with a prosperous-looking gold-mine president and told him my business. He told me his position and added, "I never saw you before and have nothing against you personally. But professionally you are my enemy, for if you succeed you will spoil my labor market."

Fortunately such men are the exception, and co-operation is the general rule. But so far as the illiterates are concerned, there are *no* exceptions.

Chapter 6

I Remember!

During the last twenty years there have been, not dozens nor hundreds, but thousands of evidences of the wistful eagerness of illiterates to read.

There rises before my memory the enormous campaign in Bihar Province, India, where Moslems and Hindus forgot their antipathy and taught one another. I saw school buildings and homes crowded with eager learners. At Gaya jail fifteen hundred prisoners were teaching one another, and as I came in they treated me like a god from heaven. While other prisoners and the warden wept, the poet of the prison recited a long poem containing these lines:

The Spring season has set in for our souls.
The name of God has a new sweetness.
The garden of my heart has blossomed forth with new
beauty.
Praise be to God for the exceeding grace He has shown
to us in prison.
The days of our sighs and groans are over and a new
song is on our lips.
We were in a prison of the mind long before we came
to this jail.

Today there is a new longing in our hearts.

India has been living in a dungeon of ignorance, but now the good news has reached us that the day of her emancipation is dawning.

No longer shall we be slaves of midnight ignorance.

Who am I, that I dare to dream the incredible new aspirations which fill my soul!

I remember Baroda State, where a thousand people led by an Indian Scottish bagpipe band met me at the station before daybreak and before I was up, and marched to a great *mala* or carnival, where they celebrated all day long the opening of many blind eyes.

I remember teaching two hundred prostitutes in Dar Es Salaam to read, women who had been forced into evil life and wanted to get out of it, and hoped that literacy was the door to decency and health. I remember their courtesy, their reverence, their gratitude.

I remember a man who came for many days to the nurse in Wembo Nyama to have "an injection for ignorance"; how he laughed and trembled when the nurse brought him to me for his first triumphant recitation!

I remember a hundred new literates looking happy as angels when we gave them their diplomas in Wembo Nyama; I remember that one old man in a class became hysterical when he found he could learn, and giggled and shouted like one gone crazy, so that we had to stop the class! He couldn't endure his bliss! Mary Hurlburt tells of a man who came to her, saying, "I want the book that makes the blind to see."

I remember in Kessua little boys and girls teaching their fathers and mothers, and bringing them up for their diplomas, while the crowd applauded and the parents wiped their eyes.

I remember old women in Blantyre, Nyasaland, growing so hysterical with delight at the end of the first easy lesson that they danced round and round, shaking hands with everybody in the church in uncontrollable rapture.

I remember the look of heavenly joy on the faces of the 396 who received their diplomas at Donde after studying the "each one teach one" way. I remember how, after I had examined one woman and passed her, she suddenly threw her arms around the man who had taught her, and cried in a flood of tears, "You taught me to read, you taught me, you taught me!"

I remember thousands of students who had learned to read in Uganda and who erected booths of reeds and bulrushes to welcome the man who had helped make their lessons. I remember the presents they gave me out of their poverty. Many dozens of eggs, pineapples, chickens, roosters, and one huge sheep.

I remember the ten men and women whom we had taught their first lesson in Guatemala City, bursting out in tears of joy at the church service because at last they would be able to read the Bible, and all the congregation, including myself, weeping with them.

I remember the old Maya woman in Yucatan, when I told her that she would make a good teacher, burying her head in her arms and shaking with sobs. When I asked her what she was crying about, she said:

"I don't see why you came down here to teach a nobody like me. I'm nobody. What do you want?" Then she wept harder than ever.

Through my interpreter I told her:

"I don't want anything, but I learned to teach people from Jesus. He spent all His time helping people. Every minute of His day He looked for people to heal, to open their blind eyes, to feed them if they were hungry, to save them from sin, to teach them the most beautiful things in the whole world. I want you to know Jesus. When you finish this book you will be able to read His wonderful life."

She said to my interpreter: "Tell him I think Jesus is very kind."

I remember an incident in Nigeria, teaching a hundred Moslems all dressed in white. At the end of the lesson, to my consternation, they all fell down on their faces in front of me to show their gratitude. I thought of Paul and Barnabas at Lystra, and said to the interpreter, "Tell them to get up. I want to shake hands with them in the good American fashion."

I remember making and experimenting with lessons in Tanganyika with Beryl Long and her illiterate women, with babies tied on their backs. Months later Beryl Long went to a village where nobody had ever heard the gospel and began to teach the first old man who came along. He was so gleeful at learning so swiftly that he laughed and shouted with joy, and the whole village came out to share the happy miracle. Beryl Long then talked to them about Jesus. The next time she went to the village she was met by the chief at the head of the whole village.

"We have a nice room for you and we want a teacher and we are going to build a church and we all want to be Christians."

Beryl Long replied, "It takes a great deal more to be a Christian than building a church and learning to read. You have to stop all your bad customs."

The chief replied, "We have talked over all that, and we are ready to obey everything your religion demands, if only you will teach us to read."

I remember one hundred women, half of them quite old women, in Taigu, Korea, who spent a week being taught by girls from the Mission School. At the end of the week we gave them little diplomas, as we always do. Then these women began to rise spontaneously one by one to tell how they felt. One woman said, "People always called me stupid. But I learned to read and now I'll go home and read to them."

Another said, "I have stayed in this church all week, studying whenever there was any light. Now I can read the Bible, and I thank the Lord for sending you."

An old woman who looked at least eighty stood up and said, "I never had any paper of any kind, and I never believed that in my old age I would read the Bible." Then she walked up to me and said, "In the name of the Father and the Son and the Holy Ghost, I bless you."

That blessing meant everything to the Koreans, for they hold old women in great reverence and obey whatever they command.

I remember churches full of men and women in Jos, Nigeria, wearing nothing but a handful of fresh leaves, studying with zeal, and learning amazingly well. I remember their animated faces, the light in their eyes, their look of triumph, as they took their first steps out of total illiteracy. These people were real Christians, and the missionaries had been wise enough not to insist upon clothes.

I remember the women studying with enormous zeal in Leopoldville, Congo. When the interpreters told them at the end of three days that our party was about to leave, they suddenly began to shriek and to look so furious that I thought they would tear us to pieces. I asked the interpreter what had been said, and he replied, "They think you are going away while they are still nearly blind, and it breaks their hearts."

I said, "Tell them that the other missionaries are staying here and will teach them." But as we went out we heard them wailing and groaning. That, I realized, was the groan and wail of the world's hungry, sick, exploited, and illiterate.

I remember the ragged boy in Liberia who thrust into my hands a dime, all the money he had, to express his gratitude that we had come to save his country from ignorance.

I remember the new light that came into the eyes of lepers in the heart of India, in Siam, in Africa and Latin America, in the Philippine Islands, as they taught one another and began to read their precious hymnbooks and their Bibles. With no hope for this world, these unfortunates find their sole consolation in hope for the future life. This makes the ability to read the Bible the most precious of all gifts. I remember them weeping with joy.

I remember the Moro outlaw whom I taught in Lanao, Philippines, not knowing who he was. After we had finished the first lesson he took me over to a corner and said, "You taught me to read and you are the best friend I have in the world. I am going to do something for you. Is there anybody you want me to put out of the way?"

The Moro boys told me next day that the government was looking for him for murder, but did not know what he looked like.

I remember teaching the laborers at the wells of Pakistan, and the scores of garlands they put around my neck.

I remember, after teaching illiterates in Beira, Mozambique, how they tried to show their affection. One man said, "I feel like a dog that cannot find words to tell its gratitude, and can only wag its tail."

There is no end to these incidents. The wildest and most desperate men turn out to be good, loyal friends when you help them. They are full of gratitude, pathetically eager to follow you and be with you. Every night you have trouble getting away from them in order to sleep. These helpless multitudes will follow anybody who tries to help them. You don't have to be educated; you only have to love.

The most primitive people in the whole world live in the interior of New Guinea, the great island north of Australia. I taught the children of the cannibals who ate James Chalmers, the famous missionary, in

1901. The coast has been Christianized in the fifty years since Chalmers died, but the interior still has thousands of cannibals. Nobody can count them without getting cooked. The largest tribe is well called "Kookookookoo."

We made lessons in seventeen of the New Guinea languages, and then the government took us by plane to the interior, where there is a tribe which has decided to stop cannibalism. They say they have not eaten people for fifteen years. There is a missionary named Doering among them, and he is well named. Forty of us landed in little planes at the airfield which had been built there by the army. There were forty thousand people in that tribe, and more than a third of them came to us to learn to read. Each of us centered upon one student, as our custom is, while all the rest tried to look on and imitate what we said. At the end of a week we had taught the first forty who had ever read that language, for it had never before been written. Then we had our graduation for those forty and told them they were to teach the entire tribe. That Sunday at least fifteen thousand people swarmed on the airfield, marching, dancing, jumping, shouting, to celebrate this greatest event in their history. Their chiefs met in solemn council. Then the greatest chief of all came to tell us their decision:

"This is the new great day in our history. We like your religion because it does so much for us. We are all going to be Christians and we want you to baptize everybody here this afternoon. All except us chiefs. We are not quite ready. We are told that you do not allow a man to have more than one wife, but we have many. We can't think of any Christian way to get rid of them suddenly. But we will marry them off as fast as we can, and then we will be baptized too. We all want your religion, for it does so much to help us."

That night a chief, who had walked a week to get there, would not go home. He stayed around to urge each of us in the party to come to his area and help his people. "Nobody in our region knows what good is, and we need somebody to come and tell us how to be good." All of us had good excuses, for we were leaving the next day. But he would not leave until we promised to try to send somebody up from the coast as soon as we could. Even among the cannibals has come this strange, terrible passion to rise to a new level, this amazing gratitude when we help them, this eagerness to become Christians when they learn to read.

This is the kind of experience that has revealed to me a thousand times over that these people at the bottom of society are easy to win to Christ if we go humbly with a helping hand to lift them out of their poverty and ignorance.

CHAPTER 7

How Governments Welcome Us

Here is another cause for thanksgiving: nine out of ten of the governments where our committee has worked have been eager for our help. We went at the official or unofficial invitation of most of them. We worked in close co-operation with the departments of education in Mexico, Cuba, Haiti, Santo Domingo, Puerto Rico, Jamaica, Trinidad, British Guiana, Venezuela, Guatemala, Nicaragua, Ecuador, Peru, Paraguay, Brazil, Philippines, Australia, New Guinea, Republic of Indonesia, Ceylon, all the provinces and presidencies and states of India, Pakistan, Iran, Iraq, Lebanon, Turkey, Egypt, Ethiopia, Kenya, Tanganyika, Uganda, Congo, Nyasaland, North and South Rhodesia, South Africa, French Cameroons, Angola, Nigeria, Gold Coast, Liberia, Sierra Leone, Korea, Thailand, Hawaii, Basutoland, Natal, Zanzibar. In China, James Yen and Hugh Hubbard and many others have worked in constant co-operation with the government, or in its employ. This number will be larger before you read these pages, for we have invitations from five other countries which we hope to accept this year.

We were entertained by governors and kings and presidents in many of these countries, our expenses paid in whole or in part in many of them—all the way around the world by air—by one of the governments.

Not a single government in any country we have visited has done anything to prevent Christians from teaching people to read and witnessing for Christ while teaching. Thus we have an enormous advantage over the Communists, who are suspected by all governments and outlawed by many.

I have asked a great many officials why they have shown such hospitality and co-operation in teaching the illiterates, and the first reply they give is that they regard illiteracy as Enemy Number One to their progress. They cannot have technical industries of a high order with illiterate workmen. But they usually add what I think gives them the real sense of urgency. They say that the Communists have been infiltrating all through their country, stirring up the hatred of the people against the government. "The Communists say they made Russia literate and promise to make this country literate. The people want to come up and believe education is necessary, so we are taking the best steps we know to satisfy that demand."

Thus the Communists have stirred up the desire, and we fulfill it! If we go and help the world, the Communists help us, without intending to do so. The Communists are dangerous to us *only* if we fail to be Christian enough to help the world, and in that case the wrath of God, too, is dangerous. We have nothing to fear *except our failure to heed the call of anguish*.

Somebody has said that "the greatest of all sins is

indifference." Right! And it is also the greatest of all *dangers* to the United States. Our chief enemy is our indifferent selves.

There is an old saying that "you can't eat your cake and have it too." Well, you can't turn your back on the world's cry for help and get away with it.

America is the millionaire of the world, with a large part of the world's wealth. My illiterates are jealous of that when they are hungry and see us ride by in our cars and airplanes. I understand that, for whenever a millionaire turns a cold ear to my pleas to help those hungry people, I have to summon up all my Christian grace to keep my temper. Everybody despises a mean man, especially a rich mean man. America is the world's millionaire, and she decides now whether she shall be loved or scorned. Everybody loves the Rockefeller Foundation, because it helps everybody.

Pardon me if I spell this out in simple language. I do it for that large number of Americans who have never been within a thousand miles of these hungry masses and cannot comprehend even the ABC's of the world problem. By those ABC's I mean millions of humans who are hungry; their bones ache with fever, they are driven to work when they are sick, the moneylenders and landlords oppress them, and they want help. *We neglected them*, and the Communists, out to capture the world, went to these people promising not Marxian Socialism but the *American* way of life—with private ownership of land and freedom. These ignorant people believed those promises, not knowing that the final goal of Communism is government confiscation of all land and destruction of all freedom. The Communists will capture the rest of the world *unless* America awakens and actually *gives* what the Communists *promise*.

My experience is that sharing technical know-how not only makes friends, but also bears a large, early fruitage. Let us see what the countries have done where our World Literacy Committee has assisted as consultant or organizer.

In Mexico the great Christian leader Baez Camargo made a set of literacy lessons in 1940. Partly as a result of this and of our visits to Mexico between 1941 and 1944, the government adopted fine phonetic lessons and effective methods. Under Dr. Jaime Torres Bodet as Minister of Education, every person who could read was required to teach, all who could not read were required to learn, and those who failed to teach or study were fined.

A million a year have been learning to read for the past five years. Dr. Jaime Torres Bodet has been made President of UNESCO as a result of this achievement.

Cuba adopted a set of our Spanish lessons, which the *Reader's Digest* published, and is carrying on a vigorous mission campaign.

Haiti had a campaign conducted first by the Rev. Ormonde McConnell, then promoted by Ambassador White of the United States, then taken over by the Haitian Government. I saw thousands of people learning. The lessons used were in the native Haitian Creole, which is spoken by all the people. UNESCO now has a model experiment in adult education in Haiti.

A young dynamic Council of Education took our plans in Venezuela and has been carrying on a vigorous literacy program ever since.

In Ecuador, Alan Reed effectively poured his vigor and tremendous personal influence into the literacy campaign in that country. In Ecuador, one is required by law to teach if he can read, to learn if he can't read, or to pay if he doesn't teach or learn.

After lessons had been used by our missionaries for some time in Peru, the government organized 30,000 teachers to teach adults as well as children.

In Paraguay, the government started training its army cadets to teach illiterates, so that they could teach all the army.

In Brazil, the Department of Education asked me to co-operate in the preparation of lessons, then organized a splendid nation-wide campaign, and reported that a half million were taught in 1950.

In the Philippines before the World War, campaigns were going on to teach adults in a dozen languages, government and missions working together.

In New Guinea, under the vigorous stimulus of the Australian government, a new powerful literacy drive is penetrating the areas which a few years ago were cannibalistic, but nearly all the work is under the direction of missionaries. The missionaries report a graduation ceremony every three weeks!

King Farouk of Egypt invited us to prepare lessons for his country. He then paid the bill for the first edition of the Primer, and called upon all who could read to teach at least one a year as a patriotic service.

Two Egyptian Christians went down through Egypt, calling all Christians together and saying:

"King Farouk asked us to teach one a year as a patriotic service. Nearly all of us can read. Let's teach Moslems to read and tell them we are doing it for the love of Jesus. The king will be glad if we help him make Egypt literate."

The Christians of Egypt have been teaching and witnessing for Christ, and the government has never expressed any objection. Christian Egyptians now have a marvelous campaign for Arab refugees at Gaza.

No country has ever officially objected to this individual teaching and witnessing at home. My experience is that if you selflessly help the government with any felt need it loves you and appreciates your religion. If you can help them, but refuse, they hate both you and your religion.

Three-fourths of the provinces and presidencies and states of India have conducted literacy campaigns since our first visits in 1935, some provinces with tremendous zeal, and millions of people have learned to read. The government reports that illiteracy dropped from 92 per cent in 1920 to 85 per cent in 1950, which would mean that thirty-four millions had learned to read.

India, like many other governments, is opposed to any direct attempt to proselytize the people, but is eager for us to come and help them teach illiterates.

This is a most important field—indeed one of the most important in the world today.

Mahatma Gandhi emphatically and repeatedly said that while he welcomed missionaries who helped India with their needs as the Quakers do, he did not like the missionaries who spent their whole time trying to convert Hindus to Christianity. This is still the attitude of the government of India.

The government of Pakistan is putting forth desperate efforts to teach her people Urdu, with its difficult Arabic alphabet. When I visited Pakistan last year, after a ten-year absence, they were in the midst of a tremendous effort to eliminate illiteracy. They nearly killed me with hard work, praise, and kindness. Moslems are wonderful brothers the world over when they believe in your unselfish desires to help them.

Since our visit to Iran, the government has been carrying on an active literacy campaign under the direction of the army.

Lebanon, since our first visit in 1935, has made steady advances in literacy, most of the program centering around the American University.

Turkey is working tirelessly at her literacy program with large success. Dr. J. Kingsley Birge and other missionaries have made valued contributions to the government program.

Uganda, adopting the methods which we developed for Africa, is conducting a really great campaign under the direction of the Department of Education, and many thousands are learning every year.

The government of North Rhodesia, in co-operation with Mrs. Hope Hay, a missionary, has made remarkable progress. South Africa has a similar semiofficial literacy campaign under Mrs. Quintin Whyte, of the South African Institute of Race Relations.

The government of Korea, strongly supported by the American Embassy, started a good campaign in co-operation with missions during the one year between our visit and the invasion by North Korea. The American Embassy paid for the printing of the lessons.

The government of Siam engaged us to prepare their textbooks for adult illiterates, printed the books we helped prepare, and is getting teachers trained in many places.

Other countries have started so recently that there is as yet no unusual information to report. As a rule, two years after making the first experimental lessons the governments and missions are producing substantial results.

After seeing these successes, neighboring countries are inviting us three times as rapidly as our committee can respond. We plan this year to accept invitations from Algeria, Tripoli, India, Afghanistan, Burma, and the Indonesian Republic to work where we have never worked before.

Chapter 8

Literacy Makes Hungry Minds

As soon as the illiterates learn to read, another door swings open. It is the opportunity to furnish these millions of hungry minds with something good and interesting to read.

This is another open door for anybody else who wishes to enter.

It is a very, very large opportunity, for about ten million adults are learning to read each year—the number is impossible to give except in such round numbers. We know that over one hundred and fifty millions outside Russia have learned in the past three decades.

We were caught wholly unprepared to enter that literature door. The reading matter for new literates did not exist. Almost none of the literature printed in most countries is down on their level, except books and papers meant for little children. But adults are not children; they do not want children's fairy tales. They want adult ideas told in language which they can understand, just as you would if you tried to read a book in some foreign language like Greek or Hebrew having an alphabet with which you were not very familiar. You would want the matter to be interesting, but with short simple sentences and familiar words.

Until the last thirty years the literature in illiterate countries has been written to meet the exacting demands of scholars, with a beautiful and classical vocabulary; half of it is unfamiliar to new literates. Even the Bible was written far above the heads of the semi-literates. This was true in all the languages of Asia, in Spanish, Portuguese, and Italian, Arabic, and the Ethiopian languages. It was not quite so true of the African and other languages which have been reduced to writing by the missionaries in the past hundred years, but even in these tongues the reading matter was too difficult for those who have just emerged from illiteracy. And nine-tenths of it was as dull as a government bulletin!

So here are millions upon millions of people for whom a wholly new literature must be created. As yet there is little literature easy enough for them to read, and in many languages next to nothing!

The Communists saw this new open door and were prepared by experience in their own country to enter it. A hundred million people in Russia who had emerged from illiteracy could not read difficult matter, so nobody in Russia today writes for scholars. Russian style always has been simple and direct, like that of Tolstoy, but now the writers of Communist literature are far simpler than Russian writers had ever been before.

So the Russians know what it means to write for

new literatures in Asia, Africa, and Latin America. Most of China was captured by propaganda without firing a gun. Mao Tse-tung published an article in the Calcutta *Nation* while we were in India last year, which shows how this was done. He says:

The Chinese Communists have two armies, one with guns and one with pens. The army of writers is at least as important as the army of soldiers. They write for the peasants, the soldiers, the laborers, and the petty shopkeepers. They do not try to write to please the scholars! Their writers go down among the masses, live and suffer with them, learn their emotions and their needs, and write to show how Communism is the answer to their heart's desires.

That is the substance of Mao Tse-tung's article.

There are millions of posters, profusely illustrated. There are tens of millions of handbills. We have samples of them in our office as I write. The pamphlets and booklets, all far, far simpler than the former literature, are within the reading vocabulary of the fifty millions of Chinese who have learned to read in the past thirty years.

Laura Cross, quoting a Communist leader from Peking on June 21, 1950, said:

The new literature in China is quite different from the old. It's all directed toward the masses and is full of propaganda and says the same thing over and over to be sure that even the most illiterate grasps the idea. . . . They don't know how to write artistically, but they have virility and creativity. At present the sophisticated may have to be bored but the masses must be educated.

What the Communists are doing in India is evident in this letter from Madras:

> Outside the Buckingham and Carnatic Mills, before work in the early morning, during the tiffin hour, and again in the evening, you may see hundreds and even thousands of workers sitting around in groups of from twenty to a hundred, listening to one of their members reading Communist literature. The slogan seems to be that every literate is a possible agent. He may not be able to get up and make a speech, but he can read aloud to his companions the literature we supply. There is no doubt about the effectiveness of this method, and it is less costly than any other.[*]

The same sort of simple Communist reading matter has the governments of Asia and Africa worried. A missionary recently returned from Kenya Colony, saying they are excited about the quantity of Communist revolutionary propaganda they found in that colony. No country in Africa except Liberia is wholly free from fear of Communist propaganda. In Nigeria, the British government is torn between the desire to help the people read and the fear that it will help the Communists to spread the literature of violence and revolution.

The governor of Nigeria and Lord Healey invited me to a conference on their baffling dilemma in Nigeria. I told them what I believe to be the whole truth in a nutshell:

"If you try to suppress literacy, you prove that Zik is right, and you will have to fight a bloody revolu-

[*] Mr. W. H. Warren quoted this example in his talk to the Christian Literature Council on September 22, 1950.

tion. If you encourage literacy, and do little about literature, you will play perfectly into the hands of Communist agitators. The only sound plan is for you to send to England for some of the best journalists you have, bring them to Nigeria, seek Christian writers, train them to write simply and readably, have many workshops where they will write what the people want and need to read, literature showing the people how you really are helping them up to a higher level, and how Communism is lying to them. You in England have had the greatest writers in the history of the world, and you still lead all other nations. If you put your mind to it, you can easily outwrite this Communist who has no training in journalism. England ought to be ashamed of herself to be frightened by the Communist propaganda."

This is what I say of America and the entire West. We are cowards to fear the propaganda of Russia. What we do need to fear is our own inaction. Her propaganda is not within a thousand miles of the high quality of our own advertising agencies. But see where we pour all our genius! Into trying to sell automobiles and razor blades and beer to one another! Almost none of our genius has been invested in selling the ideals of Christianity and freedom and justice and honor to the other side of the world. We are losing the world just as the hare in Æsop's fable lost the race with the tortoise, by going to sleep, with stupid overconfidence and indifference. America suffers from the rabbit's swelled head. While we all slumbered and slept, the Communists came and nearly captured the world. They did not *beat* our journalists and advertising geniuses, for we never even entered the race! They won by default.

We have cornered a large part of the world's wealth, and we can't find enough ways to squander it. We have the talent, the education, the technical skills to push the Communist writers right off the map. We have been too stupid to be ashamed of ourselves! That we shall stop being such fools at once is the most crucial issue for America and for the world. Otherwise we shall not deserve to survive or be free men. We are being tried in the balances and found wanting.

If this makes you angry, don't be angry with me. I don't want us to be this way. Be angry with the way you have given pennies when you should have given dollars. Be angry because you gave your abilities to sell cigarettes, when you should have been selling freedom.

Why do not the American publishers provide this immense volume of simple literature? Because it is so relatively unprofitable. Businessmen want quick returns for their money, and in foreign countries large returns to compensate for large risks.

Why, then, doesn't our government undertake the task as the Moscow government does? We have worked ourselves up into a great fear of government doing too much, lest it become socialistic or bureaucratic.

I think the devil must laugh at this! When it comes to war preparation we let the government have a third of our national income, not learning the lesson of history, that good government is always destroyed by overtopping military power, never by any other kind of power. We are in danger of becoming a military dictatorship, and there is no danger of our becoming any other kind of dictatorship.

Still, I am not arguing for the government to control our books and magazines and newspapers abroad. I don't believe it should print what most needs to be printed. I believe in private enterprise to do this work, if the right private enterprise does it. *The right enterprise is the Christian Church,* as I hope to show in the next chapter, because it is free from the profit motive, possesses abundant resources, and has at its center the spirit of Jesus—the highest ideals the world ever saw, the only hope of real, just peace.

But before we begin that chapter let me say something about radio and television, which many people imagine are cheap, quick ways to get truth to the world. A great many people seem to think that if we can have a bigger military establishment than Russia, and can shout over the radio louder than she does, we shall be able to save the world from going Communistic and that we may even sow revolution behind the Iron Curtain.

We are spending more on the Voice of America and Crusade for Freedom radio plan than on all missions put together. It is very important. Yet it would be blind folly to depend upon it to go far in winning the cold war. First of all, it cannot get far behind the Iron Curtain, because short-wave radios are forbidden, and the others are jammed the moment they are anti-Communist. The clever Politburo knows how to keep its curtain tight.

The Voice of America thought Russia would like

to hear one of Mr. Malik's speeches in the Assembly of the United Nations. But Russia jammed it all, so her people could not even hear what was in their own favor!

Nor does the radio reach the two-thirds who are wretchedly poor and hungry, because they have no radios. My billion illiterates do not even have chairs, or beds, or tables, or knives, or forks, not to mention radios. We might set up radios in every village for the whole population to hear, but all we said would be nullified by the explanations of the Communist propagandists who circulate among those people.

I say the illiterates cannot buy radios. But when we teach them to read we have put radios in their heads! We put them there free of charge; after that all we need to do is to have our writers living among them speak their simple language on the printed page and plant in their minds what we want to grow there. One of the fortunate things about new readers is that at first they believe everything they read. They do not know that people can print lies—that's why Communism is flourishing. This tendency to believe is fortunate for us if we are doing the printing, and terrible if the Communists are doing it. We need not fear the Communists if both they and we are doing it, and if we are *really helping* the people to better things, while the Communists raise false hopes they cannot fulfill. As soon as the Church comes awake, the two things she will need to do to help the world out of its misery are to help it help itself, and then to tell the *whole truth*.

Literacy is building a bridge to ten million minds a year. We have got to cross that bridge.

You may say, "Stop literacy," but that is folly. If the missions stopped it, governments would still be teaching ten million a year. Nothing can stop it now. We cannot destroy that bridge, but we can cross it with a great army of books and papers.

CHAPTER 9

How Foreign Missions Plan for Literacy and Literature

In January 1950 the Foreign Missions Conference, at its annual meeting, took the following action to enter these two stupendous new doors, the door of literacy and the door of Christian literature.

Whereas we recognize:

The increasing eagerness of the world's illiterates to learn to read;

The requests of many governments for our help in their adult literacy campaigns;

The opportunities which we have for effective evangelism as we teach illiterates;

The near monopoly which missionaries have in training and ability in adult literacy and translation work;

The resources in men and means which American Protestants have for advancing the world cause of literacy;

The heavy responsibility which we have for supplying Christian literature to the millions who are annually becoming newly literate;

Resolved:

1. That we recommend to each member board that it select one or more missionaries to be trained in the techniques of teaching adults to read so that they in turn may teach others, both missionaries and nationals, and thus by continued repetition of this process, this invaluable means of evangelism may be brought within the reach of the widest possible circle of workers.

2. That we also recommend the selection and advanced training of missionaries and nationals gifted in the creation of Christian literature.

3. That we urge the necessary additional support of the program of the Committee on World Literacy and Christian Literature serving all the Area Committees of the Foreign Missions Conference, in order to take advantage of the opportunities thus created.

This dull, innocent-sounding motion is packed with dynamite, if you know what it implies. It means that the mission boards adopted the program which the World Literacy Committee proposed at the conference. If you wish to read that proposal, it is printed in full under the title *Literacy as Evangelism.*

Briefly the plan is this:

We plan as swiftly as possible to train *all* missionaries in the "each one teach and win one" method so that they can go out to teach and win native Christians: *each one to teach and win one.* Millions of the non-Christians of the world are illiterate. In fact, before the Protestant Reformation, ninety-five per cent of the whole world was illiterate. The Reformation placed enormous emphasis upon the reading of the Bible, and out of that drive came a belief in universal education for rich and poor alike. In this twentieth century, belief in mass education has taken hold of most of the world. Nine-tenths of the nations representing *every religion* are now making plans for universal education for adults as well as for children. All the illiterate peoples of the world clamor for it.

This is what missions see now, and they are determined to help the program because it is Christian, because it opens the Bible, and because it wins friends for Christ.

Our committee has established courses in the art of "each one teach one" in Hartford Seminary and in Scarritt College, Nashville. But this reaches only scores, while we need to train ten thousand as fast as possible. Time is running out. Every mission board is beginning to train picked missionaries to go out to train *all* the missionaries of its denomination.

But this also is too slow. So a correspondence course is now planned which we hope to send to *every* missionary in the world.

Our plan is to mobilize as swiftly as possible all the native Christians in the non-Christian areas into armies for teaching illiterates and winning them to Christ.

There are about thirty million native Christians (about half of them Protestants and half of them Catholics) in the midst of 1200 million non-Christians, one Christian to every *forty* non-Christians. We aim to put all these native Christians to work teaching and winning their neighbors. When that is accomplished we shall be able to teach 30 million a year to read, to follow the way of love and Christ, and not the way of hate and revolution.

Theoretically, if we could train all these Christians at once and if we had as much of the Holy Spirit as was evident at Pentecost, the number would rise in something like geometric progression—30 millions teaching 30 millions the first year, 60 millions teaching the next, then 120 millions, then 240 millions, then 480 millions, then over the top! If there were no failures in the program the world would be literate in a few years, and a large percentage of the newly taught would be Christians!

Mathematically that is possible, but of course nothing like this is happening, because, for one thing, we do not have enough trained missionaries to train and direct these thirty millions. It is also true that half of those taught would fail to teach after being taught; they would lack the Christian spirit. And as for a Pentecost, experience shows that where a church is well organized so that nearly everybody teaches, a veritable Pentecost *does* fall upon that church. Then, caught up with fervor, many Christians teach and win one illiterate *a month,* and some a hundred or more a year! When they get a taste of the joy of teaching and winning, they develop an almost fanatical passion for more and more of that joy! I know how that feels—I have it!

It is not difficult to train the church members. The simple Primer is so easy to teach that they need only follow the printed lines and encourage the students, helping now and then. We also show each church member how to love and praise his students, and so win their gratitude. We say, "Never an unpleasant or discouraging moment! Never complain, or frown; never say 'no,' never ask a question the student can't answer. Look pleased and overwhelmed with admiration. Love your student and silently pray for him." It sounds like a Dale Carnegie course in salesmanship—and it works!

At the end of the lesson tell him that the Christians are teaching because Jesus wants to help other people. We have prepared a series of short stories about the kindness of Jesus, to be told during each lesson. If the teacher is a sincere Christian, the student will soon love his Christ. It is as easy for a Christlike teacher to make the student love Christ as it is to make him literate.

We set the entire church membership to work, each one to teach some neighbor at home, at any hour, until in one or two weeks the Primer is learned. Then all the students are invited to come to church and get their diplomas. As they march forward and receive their diplomas, the pastor and church officials all give them hearty congratulations—the first time they have entered a Christian church!

Then the new literates are invited to come and study the second book, *The Story of Jesus*, so that they can learn to read the Bible and books and magazines. In *The Story of Jesus* they build a vocabulary and they learn by heart what Jesus said and did.

Wherever a church follows this method, the membership of the church doubles rapidly and the whole congregation experiences a veritable outpouring of

God's spirit. One can't give away his Christian faith without getting more!

This, then, is how we are trying to mobilize an army of thirty million to spread love and peace over our distracted world.

Eric Johnston, former President of the American Chamber of Commerce, and now Economic Stabilization Administrator, returned from a recent trip around the world with the alarming tidings that the Communists have "millions of missionaries scattered through every country, converting the people to Communism." We have millions too! Thirty millions of native Christians, waiting to be trained for our army. But we lack trained missionaries and money to organize these 30,000,000 into teaching and winning regiments. We can't do it until America helps us in a big way.

America's task is to finance and train and send thousands of missionaries competent to drill and direct our unorganized and untrained army. That is a big order, but there is another just as big.

An Army of Journalists

We must provide literature for the ten millions now learning every year. We can do it. If we get our enormous potential machinery moving we can provide good, readable literature for them all.

At Syracuse University the Department of Journalism has developed a special division of Religious Journalism to teach missionaries and nationals how to write very simple readable matter for new literates.

The big problem in such a school is to find a faculty which knows enough about this simple level of writing for new literates in Asia, Africa, and Latin America. Dean Lyle Spencer of Syracuse is one of these rare professors, for he has lived and written in the Near East and many other parts of the world for many years.

But we can't wait for these young people to graduate. We can't wait! So we are interviewing hundreds of newspaper reporters responsible for religious news and inviting those with a Christian passion to come out and help train natives to write. The men and women in the newspaper business have priceless experience, they have proven that they can write, and many are ready to go as fast as we find sponsors for them.

As soon as our funds permit, we shall send these Christian journalists out to mission colleges to start schools of journalism in which natives will be taught to write far more simply and alluringly than they had dreamed possible.

These schools of journalism will also be workshops in which the students and professors study what the people want to read, and then write it for newspapers and magazines. If no newspapers exist, they will actually begin them, printing them with attractive cartoons and photographs and large clear type in the best American style. Artists in cartooning and photography will have special classes. Together they will plan and write books, and illustrate them.

The students will be taught to use the latest printing processes, which make printing so much cheaper, swifter, and more readable.

There will also be classes dealing with all the problems of promotion and sale of literature, getting it into people's homes and getting it read. So, in reality, these schools of journalism will be publishing centers as well as schools, the students learning to do by doing, which is both good education and good business.

So far, all that has been done is pitifully inadequate, hardly a beginning, as may be seen when we realize that over a hundred million semi-literate people who learned in the past two decades are starving for good, interesting literature. If I had a hundred million dollars I would invest it in meeting this need for readable uplifting and religious literature.

I would offer *any price* necessary to try to secure the finest directors of journalism to be found among our great newspapers and magazines. I would entice them from *The New York Times* and the *Reader's Digest*. I would send out an army of them to capture this field from the Communists, confident that we in America have a hundred times more of *everything* it takes to flood the world with fascinating reading matter—far more money, far more experience, far more training in keen competition, far better writers. Yet we Americans waste this genius and money in mad competition with one another, newspapers crowding one another to the wall, when a vast starving world needs us! It does not make sense. We ought to hide our heads in shame.

Does anybody want to invest a hundred million dollars for twenty years to build this bridge?

Don't you see how literacy and simple readable literature would be the bridge from those who *know how* to those who *need* to know how?

Do you want them to know how to get more production from their land? Here is your bridge!

Do you want them to have better sanitation and hygiene? Here is your bridge!

Do you want them to know about child care and motherhood? Here is your bridge!

Or home economics, or balanced diet? Here is your bridge!

Do you want to prove to them that America is their friend? Here is your bridge!

Do you want them to understand freedom? Here is your bridge!

Do you want to trade with them? Here is your advertising medium.

Foolish, shortsighted, blindly selfish America! Why don't you build that bridge while there is yet a world in which to build it?

CHAPTER 10

It Pays to Be a Good Neighbor

America has had enough experience, if we profit by it, to know that one dollar invested in being a good neighbor brings as much return as a thousand dollars invested in guns and bombs. Indeed, the good-neighbor program has been a marvelous success wherever it has been carried out by sincere, kindhearted men. It fails only when we try to substitute loans of money and to work from a distance instead of sending real warmhearted friends.

The Philippine Islands is one example. We took the Islands in 1899 without wanting them. We were at war with Spain and there was a Spanish fleet in the Philippines. Dewey sank the Spanish fleet, and the Islands were on our hands. Aguinaldo and the Filipino patriots, thinking that we were like their Spanish foes, fought us for a year. Then we sent a delegation to explain our motives. "We are here to liberate you, but we must protect you from Spain and every other greedy power, and we will set you free the moment you have a unified, strong government, and we will do our best to help you."

That delegation won over Aguinaldo. He laid down his arms, and the Philippines and America began one of the happiest experiments in the history of our country. I had the delight of sharing that experiment between 1915 and 1940, and saw how it paid to be a sincere good neighbor.

We sent a thousand school teachers to the Philippines within a year after peace came, six hundred on one boat. We have sent twenty thousand teachers altogether. Never from any other country have so many men and women of good will gone forth to help another country, asking nothing in return. One out of four died in the Philippines, but their influence will never die. We did better in every respect for the Filipinos than any other colonial power had ever done, set up a sound self-government and then set them free as our "daughter republic."

We had our payoff when the Japanese struck in southeastern Asia. The only country of which we were sure in all Asia during the war was the Philippine Republic. The Filipinos suffered far more casualties during the Philippine campaign than did we, had their principal cities ruined worse than any other country on the allied side, worse even than Britain, and they helped us win the war. As I write they are fighting by our side in Korea.

Carlos Romulo, Philippine Ambassador to the United States, former president of Rotary International, then a delegate to and finally President of the Assembly of the United Nations, the president under whom the Assembly was for the first time opened with a minute of silent prayer, is a magnificent product of the schools established in the Philippines under our administration.

Latin America is another example of the payoff for being a good neighbor. Before 1930 practically all Latin America hated us and feared us because of our "big-stick policy." They called us "gringos"—a word of loathing. Then Herbert Hoover, with his experience of service in Europe and his Quaker ideas, went down to Latin America, and in spite of his awkward shyness (or perhaps partly because of it) convinced Latin America that we sincerely wanted to be her good neighbor and not her boss. Franklin D. Roosevelt continued that policy with his winning friendliness. We established a department of Co-ordinators for Latin America, with Nelson Rockefeller at its head. Rockefeller worked with prodigious zeal and miraculous effectiveness to win the heart of Latin America. Most of our international firms have co-operated. In Venezuela, the oil companies espoused the principle that the oil is the property of Venezuela, and that the oil companies are entitled only to the profit they deserve for helping the government extract this wealth from the ground. On this basis both government and companies prosper, and the employes are far better treated than any others in Venezuela.

Now we have our payoff. When Communism threatens to close in on us East and West, Latin America is the one continent where we have the least to fear.

My own delightful experience in Latin America in the interests of literacy was due to this co-operation of the American Embassies and of the co-ordinators, who opened the doors of gracious hospitality to me, —a Protestant missionary working in a Roman Catholic continent. The countries welcomed me because I offered to help meet a greatly felt need.

Liberia is just now Exhibit A of our experiments in good-neighbor policy. After the Civil War of 1861–65 we sent all the freed slaves to Liberia who wanted to go, and we protected Liberia from being gobbled up by any of the foreign powers, which at one time or another took all the rest of Africa. Afterward, for a long period, we neglected Liberia, because malaria made it a deathtrap for whites; even the missionaries gave it up after losing scores of martyrs to the cause of Christ. Then medicine conquered malaria, even in Liberia. Missionaries of a dozen denominations began to work in the country, many of them black missionaries. Liberia is the only country on earth where the government officially works hand in hand with missionaries to make everybody literate, to make everybody Christian, and to make everybody speak and read English.

The U.S. government sent experts in agriculture, in health, in finance, and in education, to co-operate with the Liberian government.

President Tubman has left nothing to be desired in appreciation and co-operation. Harvey Firestone established a great rubber plantation in Liberia, paying the workers good wages and giving them good home conditions. The Firestone plantation is now erecting a great medical and research center in Liberia, with the purpose of defeating malaria, sleeping sickness, dysentery, yellow fever, venereal disease, hookworm, and many other diseases which make Africa the most unhealthy continent in the world.

The Firestone Company also proposes to co-operate with the government and mission literacy program to teach all its employes to read and speak the English language.

Then Stettinius organized a company to develop the tremendous iron and gold and other resources of the country, offering excellent working conditions and wages to the men, and placing the welfare of Liberia at the very top of their objectives. Liberia in the last two years has become the miracle of the world. It is the only country in all Africa which has no fear of Communism.

Two years ago in India, I ran across another striking instance of how it pays to be a good neighbor. After India and Pakistan were set free, there were frightful riots in India. Millions of Moslems fled from India to Pakistan, and millions of Hindus fled from Pakistan to India. Strewn along the highways were countless thousands, wounded, hungry, cold, and wretched. It happened that there was in India an abundance of medicine, food, and clothing which had never been sent "over the hump" to China, because the war with Japan ended so suddenly. So Christians and missionaries, dropping their other work, began binding up the wounded refugees, feeding the hungry, and clothing the naked. In two weeks, Christianity was so popular that Moslems wore Christian crosses to deceive the Hindus, and Hindus wore crosses so that they would not be killed by the Moslems!

Japan is one of the most striking illustrations in the world of how a nation can change from hate to love in two years. At the end of World War II, they hated us bitterly. Then MacArthur, who understood Japan, instead of punishing the Japanese, did his best to give them good government and to help them recover. His kindness was so surprising that public opinion turned a somersault. When a vote was taken in 1949 to determine what nation was most popular among the Japanese, the United States got ten times as many votes as any other nation and more than all the others put together. It paid to be a good neighbor to Japan.

But had we stayed away and merely loaned Japan a billion dollars, as we have often done for other countries, she would not have loved us. A good neighbor doesn't lend money; a good neighbor goes and lends a hand. Moneylenders are never loved.

Chapter 11

Technical Aid

For ten years I have been preaching to such Americans as will come to listen to a missionary that our losing the world to Communism is our own fault, wholly because we are blind to the situation, imagining that we can have a wonderful America and let the rest take care of themselves as we take care of ourselves. I wrote that point of view in the last chapter of *The Silent Billion Speak*. Old, blind ex-Senator Owen of Oklahoma had this book read to him, and it set his soul on fire. He distributed it to all the senators. One of the senators who read it was Senator Harry Truman.

Four years ago, tingling with my experiences with the illiterates who were passionately eager to learn to read, and with the astonishing reception which governments were giving a humble missionary who happened to have something they wanted, I was telling the story in a church in New York City. The pastor's wife, a woman of intense Christian devotion, caught fire with this vision. She telephoned a well known statesman in Washington and told him she wanted President Truman to hear this story personally from me. A few days later her husband, the statesman and I went into the office of President Truman, while the pastor's wife sat outside and prayed. This was a real opportunity to present my message. We said in substance:

"President Truman, the world is swiftly falling before Communist propaganda, because it is hungry and sick and unhappy and desperately determined to come up out of its misery. Our experience with literacy shows us that anybody who goes out with something those people need and offers to help them has their love and gratitude. The Communists are winning them by telling them we don't care, and by promising to help them. We believe, Mr. President, that if you would tell the world that America stands ready to help all nations help themselves by sharing our technical knowledge unselfishly, you would find the world wildly enthusiastic. You could win the cold war if you kept that promise."

The President listened with close attention for perhaps twenty minutes. Then he said this thing we proposed was religion. He wondered whether America would follow him if he made such a promise. Then he said, "You men go out and start a revival. I am a great believer in religion. Nothing but religion will stir a nation to rise to the high ideal you have proposed today." The President made no promises.

But many other people were telling the President the same thing we had told him. Among these was the famous Dr. Norris Dodd, the agricultural expert who, under the United States government and the United

Nations, has been helping countries all over the planet raise better crops. It is probable that President Truman has been thinking about this matter for many years, always wondering whether America had enough religion to go out unselfishly to lift the world out of its dangerous misery. He wanted to be sure he could take the country with him.

What was our delight when, on January 20, 1949, in the midst of an inaugural address of the usual order, President Truman electrified the world by his now famous Point IV. The President said:

> We must embark on a bold new program for making the benefits of our scientific advances and industrial progress available for the improvement and growth of undeveloped areas. . . .
>
> Our aim should be to help the free peoples of the world, through their own efforts, to produce more food, more clothing, more materials for housing, and more mechanical power to lighten their burdens. . . .
>
> The old imperialism—exploitation for foreign profit —has no place in our plans. What we envisage is . . . democratic fair-dealing.
>
> Only by helping the least fortunate of its members to help themselves can the human family achieve the dooont, satisfying life that is the right of all people. . . .

This is Point IV!

Whatever happens to Harry Truman, he will go down in history as the first Chief Executive of any nation who ever proposed such a world-wide Christian plan. It proposes to lift four-fifths of the human race above the line of hunger and despair, not by violence and revolution and liquidation, but by unselfishly sharing our knowledge and our abundance.

The reaction to the President's proposal in America was lukewarm. Some Americans took sides mildly for or against the idea, but most Americans were uncertain and neutral. They did not know what to make of it.

But the rest of the world was not lukewarm—it was hot. Other nations were more enthusiastic about Point IV than about anything else since the United Nations began. I was in Siam and saw in huge letters across the first page of a newspaper, "America Promises to Help All Needy Nations." People were amazed and thrilled. Point IV had shot new hope into the veins of the disintegrating world.

The United Nations was electrified. On November 15, 1950, the nations voted unanimously, no country absenting, to invest many millions of dollars in aiding the underdeveloped areas with their technical skills. No action of the United Nations ever received a larger number of votes.

Both the United States government and the United Nations have worked vigorously to carry out their proposals. There are many books and hundreds of bulletins and pamphlets dealing with the subject. Documents on Point IV may be obtained from the United States government or from the United Nations.

Harper & Brothers recently published a book entitled *Bold New Program*, by Willard R. Espy, of *Reader's Digest*, which now is obtainable in a twenty-five cent edition. The Public Affairs Institute at Washington also has published a series of pamphlets under the same general title.

No nation dares be against helping the world, and not many individuals have dared to oppose it. Some businessmen have expressed fear of teaching other people arts and sciences which will enable them to compete with our own business enterprises, as Japan was doing before the second World War. Most businessmen believe, on the other hand, that if other countries have more industries they will be able to buy far more from the United States. Helping the other people of the world help themselves is in the long run very far-sighted good business.

The chief difference of opinion is as to how much of Point IV the government should undertake, and how much should be left to private enterprise. The American Merchants Association issued a brochure saying it would support the Point IV idea only if it were all left to private enterprise. The Association for Economic Education, with more than a million dollars back of it, has also come out for a private-enterprise Point IV.

The two obvious reasons for this are: first, business wants to get all the profits it can, with no government competition; and, second, there is a very widespread opposition to allowing any more power to drift into the hands of the government. Americans want just as little government as possible, except when threatened by war. So far, President Truman has received from Congress only 26 million of the 45 million dollars he asked, and consequently the United Nations got much less from the United States than it had expected.

So—if the government will not do it adequately, who *will?*

Private enterprise ought to be given a chance to do all it *will.* But there are several most important needs which business will not help because there is no profit to be made in helping those needs.

For example, private enterprise seldom invests in education, because it is usually a financial loss. For the same reason business seldom invests in health. It seldom invests in home economics, or dietetics, or ideal home life, or child care, or simple agriculture, because these produce no immediate profits.

It is true that some international business concerns do help education and health in some countries in a magnificent way. I have already mentioned the Firestone Company building a great medical center for Liberia. The oil companies in East Arabia have started notable schools. Such companies see that it pays to purchase good will. But the list of those who invest large sums abroad with no prospect of return is short.

Private philanthropies have been a great blessing. We have had marvelous results in health and education from the Rockefeller and Carnegie foundations. Happily, many fortunes are being converted into foundations to prevent them from disappearing as inheritance taxes. There is reason to believe that *some* of the newer foundations will see the vision of service abroad. It seems likely that a much larger proportion of the gifts of these foundations will be spent abroad for lifting the backward people than in the past. Some of them see now that one dollar spent abroad does more for saving the peace than a hundred dollars spent in America, just because the battlefield of the world is among the hungry and discontented multitudes.

President Truman's appointment of Nelson Rockefeller at the head of a strong committee gives strength to the Point IV program. As head of the Co-ordinators in Latin America, Nelson Rockefeller was a tremendous success. He has indeed been rightfully called a "one-man Point IV for South America." He will command the confidence of the philanthropies, will enlist the aid of international business, and so will be able to bring together these powerful units to co-operate with government in an all-out American effort to lift the world.

Americans must see just what a good Point IV is *not*. It is *not* charity, in the sense of giving away our surplus food or old clothes. In an earthquake or famine or revolt or after a tragedy like that in Korea it is necessary to feed the hungry and clothe the naked. People do not want to remain paupers; they want to catch up with us so that they will not need our charity. No beggar ever really thanks the man who gives him alms. The gift leaves the benefactor with a glow of virtue, but it humiliates the recipient. People want us to help them *to help themselves* so that they will not need charity and can be independent and self-respecting.

This does not mean that we should continue to destroy potatoes and oranges and other crops instead of giving them away. One of the most stinging accusations the Communists can use to make the hungry people hate us is to tell them that we destroy a hundred times as much food as we give to feed the poor. One of the things Mr. Nehru found it hardest to forgive was that we refused to release for India some fifteen shiploads of wheat which were lying in New York Harbor while the wheat molded. We are making people hate us when we destroy food. The Communists are seeing to that.

Most of my readers have heard a Russian delegate talking over the radio from the United Nations. He may not like me if I say that he is the most diabolically clever liar since Adolf Hitler. His attempt to make the ignorant world believe that South Koreans, led by the United States, started the Korean war by invading North Korea is an insult to every intelligent person in the world, but hundreds of millions of illiterate people, who know nothing of the facts, will believe that lie if it is repeated often enough. Day after day, Russia is telling the world that America is the Shylock of the world. No nation in history has employed lies so effectively. Our only answer is to prove that America is the Good Samaritan of the world, prove it with a million deeds. Yet—there are men in America who will fight the Point IV program unless we can exact our pound of flesh. These men in this terrible hour are playing into Russia's hands, though they bitterly hate her.

I do not mean that we should give the world all our surplus food—and stop there. That would not make them love us. I mean that we must also give the world *our best selves*, sending a hundred thousand of our finest men and women with technical skills to help people help themselves, to mingle with them democratically and with no color consciousness, to love them, to help them fulfil their aspirations, and then we ought to back these men and women with the financial resources which they need. I mean *all out*—as we fight our wars.

That and that alone will nullify the campaign of lies which is building up hate for America. Isn't this self-evident? I believe that the men who oppose Point IV will quickly endorse it when they see the facts, and that the hungry multitudes whom I know so well want to come up to self-respect where they will not need anybody's charity. They have begun to see the true meaning of democracy, and *that* is what democracy means.

We must offer our technical skills, asking neither favor nor profit in return. We must show them how to get ten times or a hundred times as much from their land as they get now. We must show them how to conquer those diseases and insects that kill their crops and animals and children. We must show them how to conquer malaria and hookworm and dysentery and venereal disease and plague. We must help them as they struggle up out of their hell. We must go to their sides and help them. There is no substitute for the real, living, loving person rubbing elbow to elbow with the people who toil.

The New York Herald Tribune for October 29, 1950, says exactly this in an article by Walter Reuther, head of the United Auto Workers. He declares that the free nations must immediately "launch a total war against poverty and social injustice . . . . Too long we have made the tragic mistake of believing that freedom's fight in Asia could be won alone on the battlefields. It is imperative that we learn the lesson and act in the knowledge that freedom's fight must be won in the rice fields. Communism did not conquer China. Communism moved in to fill the vacuum created by our failure to wage war there against poverty and hunger." Reuther is smart!

Unless we help people to help themselves, the Voice of America and the Crusade for Freedom are utterly futile as substitutes for this help. Let nobody suppose that the onward sweep of Communism is going to be stopped by any such easy short cut. I like the radio idea chiefly because it helps us to analyze our own case and see whether it really will win the hungry masses. Perhaps it may do us good, but I lie in dread lest it lull us to sleep.

I think the broadcasters realize that *abstract* truth is not enough to save us. There is one truth which Communists constantly push before the destitute masses. This is that they are desperately hungry, while America is fabulously rich, and wasting more than they ever get to eat or wear. That is an ugly truth. If you talk over the radio to the hungry man about the danger of being enslaved to Russia and about the glory of democracy and freedom, he will shake his fist at that radio and ask, "Freedom from what? Freedom from hunger? What are you doing about it? There is no way up but to kill the landlords and destroy the government." As Espy puts it, "They cannot eat democracy." But the broadcaster cannot hear what the hungry masses say to him at their radios and what their Communist comrades sitting among them in every village say when they hear our broadcasts. But I know! And it isn't sweet. You cannot counteract Communism by absent treatment.

If we fail to help those masses, all the radio talk in the world will make them hate us more. Words as a substitute for deeds are loathsome to hungry people. Their landlords have always used mealy-mouthed lies about "legal right" to cover their oppression. Genuine help alone will prove that we are sincere and that the Communists are telling lies about us. For the masses will be deeply suspicious until we prove our genuineness.

But our wealth need not be a hindrance to us. If we use that wealth wisely to help the world help itself to be wealthy also, if we use it to send technicians to help those people help themselves to our level, our wealth can be our salvation.

If we help those people to a new higher level above poverty, above sickness, above exploitation and oppression, as the Communists promise to do, then our broadcasts will become irresistible! We shall have a truth to tell them which will silence the lies and half-truths of the Communists. Deeds—compassionate helpfulness plus witness, these two—will save the world if they are done by men who love their fellow men. And this is pure Christlikeness. That is why the Church should take the leading part, because only Christians can do this with perfectly Christian love.

CHAPTER 12

What Could Be Done

This chapter should be written by engineers, human engineers and doctors. I have neither the training nor the time to make the great research which an adequate picture would require.

One thing we must keep in mind. We are aiming to help hungry people, not to make the rich richer. In Egypt a great dam was built across the Nile in 1890. This enabled the Nile to triple its production. Land values soared and rents went up. The common people went heavily in debt to the moneylenders at rates of 30 per cent or higher. They lost their land. In 1941 half of Egypt's wonderful land was owned by 12,000 landlords, 442 acres each on an average; 2,280,000 peasants held an average of .8 of an acre each, and millions were landless paupers. The farm family received an average income of $36 per year—family income, not individual. That was improvement which did the hungry people harm.

We are not seeking to speed up the exploitation of the world's mineral wealth for the benefit of the few. Harold Isaacs, in *Bold New Program* Series, No. 2, **writes:**

The great gold and diamond mines and farms of South Africa . . . have been made possible by the mass dispossession and virtual enslavement of the African people. About 6,000,000 rural Africans have been pushed off their land into 40 million acres, while 800,000 whites have 204,500,000 acres, seized from the blacks by the state without compensation. Deprived of his land the African was forced to work for the whites or die . . . virtual forced labor in the mines, other industries, and on white owned farms, policed and herded, deprived of all freedom of movement, and paid from $1 to $12 a month.

This kind of "economic development" is not what Point IV must *help*—it is the thing Point IV must stop if we are to halt the onward march of Communism.

A study shows that the per capita annual income of the lower two-thirds of the human race was $41 a year; for China and Indonesia it was $22. We must lift that. The per capita income of men, women, and children in the United States was then $525.

Another study showed that the food consumption of two-thirds of humanity was 2150 calories a day, 400 calories below an adequate diet and only 300 above starvation; those who go lower die. Ours in America is 3040 a day. We eat too much!

How could we change these figures? (I do not refer to ours—we can diet!)

Norris Dodd says that if we can increase the world yield of agriculture 10 per cent and make it available to all people, there will be sufficient food for perfect health.

And we can go far above that! How can we do it? For one thing, by introducing better seeds all over the world. Where introduced, hybrid corn has already increased the production from 20 per cent to 300 per cent.

Agricultural science can perform similar miracles for every crop by using better seeds, better plows, better fertilizers, better irrigation systems, and by destroying diseases of crops. It seems to be agreed now that if we applied our agricultural know-how over the world we could increase the food supply so much that instead of 1,500 millions of the world being far below the decency level, we could support 3 billions with food to spare. We have the know-how, and need only to *show how* (Raushenbush, *Bold New Program* Series).

There are also exciting opportunities to reclaim vast areas of the world that are now arid.

Africa has a fifth of the world's surface, one-third desert, a third jungle, with high, cool plateaus. Its possibilities for development in agriculture are incalculably great. Africa has 40 per cent of the possible hydroelectric horsepower of the whole world. Less than 1 per cent is used. There are proposals to turn the water of the Niger river, the Zambesi, the Nile, the Congo, out over rich desert loam and convert enormous areas into lush tropical gardens and farms. Much of the Sahara could be covered with grass or farmed.

It looks as though for a while Africa will need engineers and irrigation and agricultural and soil-conservation experts to plan out these exciting achievements. But God grant they may be Christians, or all this development will make more misery for the

African, not less, as Egypt and South Africa reveal.

Let us look at Asia.

In Iran, where 90% of the country's 15,000,000 people are illiterate, ill-fed and ill-housed, an enlightened Shah proposes to stop the Soviet threat by breaking up his huge royal estates into small farms and selling them to their peasant operators. He suggests the same move to the wealthy landowning class which now runs the country; they will fight such a social revolution, but the Shah seems ready to push through legislation aimed at breaking up the iniquitous semi-feudal estates which *must* be broken up if the nation is to escape the Soviet noose. It is a marvelous move— "Western papers please copy!"

Iraq, next door, has an even more breath-taking program. She has an eight-man board to reconstruct the vast irrigation system which made it possible to support 30,000,000 people when Babylon was in her prime. That irrigation program is being blocked by a dispute as to who will control and exploit the water supply. That kind of thing makes the Communists gleeful.

Nobody yet knows what possibilities exist for converting the seemingly limitless level waste of Arabia into a garden. Perhaps with atomic energy we shall distill water from the oceans, just as clouds do, and make Arabia the very garden of Eden many think it once was. All this directly aims at stopping the major cause of wars in the Near East. The reason the people there are so violent and unhappy is that they are hungry. If this desert land were watered and the people could have their own acres it would easily support a multitude of happy people, one hundred times the present population. Frances Perkins, in her book on *The Roosevelt I Knew*, says that Roosevelt told her, "When I get through being President of the United States I think Eleanor and I will go to the Near East and see if we can manage to put over an operation like the Tennessee Valley system that will really make something out of that country."

One hopes Roosevelt's spirit may yet watch over that dream and make it come true.

Alas, thus far Ibn Saud of Saudi Arabia has not invested any of the billions he is receiving as royalties from American oil companies in the development of these vast areas for the welfare of the hungry multitudes. He had better do it if he wants to save Arabia from the Communists.

Look at Afghanistan. This country has never had a missionary, because it is solidly Moslem. But, awakening with the rest of the world, it invited Morrison-Knudsen, an American engineering firm, to make a plan for building roads and industries, for which they expect to spend 135 million dollars. They also employed American teachers, some of them deeply Christian men, who went with a wonderful missionary spirit—and were liked.

Palestine, now the home of the Jewish Republic of Israel, has one of the most astonishing programs in the world, which has already turned desert and rocks into a paradise, They have plans to develop the Jordan Valley which will make fertile 900,000 acres that now are arid, provide room for 2 million people and generate 500 million kilowatts of electricity. This plan was conceived by the famous American soil-conservation expert, Dr. Walter C. Lowdermilk.

The reason Palestine can carry out this program is that the Jews tithe, and so can raise 100 million dollars a year for Palestine. If the Protestants of the United States would tithe and would give half their tithe to remove hunger and despair abroad through technically trained missionaries, *they could have more than two billion dollars a year* to help the world as the Jews are helping Palestine. That would be ample! If we will not listen to our Lord and do this, we are going to listen to the threat of Communists rolling down over Asia and Africa, and perhaps over the whole of Europe.

Sam Higginbottom and his associates in the Presbyterian Agricultural College at Allahabad, India, proved that by crossbreeding, the cows of India can be made to yield far more milk. Hindus do not kill cows, so millions of useless cows are eating up India without yielding any returns. Allahabad is changing cows from liabilities to assets.

It will be possible in India to add forty million acres of rice-producing land, to save twelve million tons of rice now lost annually by poor storage methods, to improve milling and transportation and cooking, and so to make *twice as much* rice in India available for food. Yet we do not need that much to raise India above the hunger line. All we need is ten per cent!

Fortunately, the new Indian government has taken the large estates and divided them into small farms, a wise move that is the best guarantee that India will not fall under the Iron Curtain.

We must hope that by sane and patient diplomacy China may be won back to our friendship. If that happens, then America can help in the most stupendous program of social upbuilding possible on the whole earth. Dam projects now on paper could increase her electric output 115 billion kilowatt hours, equal to the *total* used by France, Germany, Russia, and the United Kingdom together! China will need it—she has a fourth of the world's population, more people than all those countries put together. Nitrogen fertilizer could be extracted from the air in sufficient quantity to fertilize 100 million sterile acres of Chinese land which were long ago worn out, and irrigation could make ten million acres of desert land rich in productivity.

As Espy puts it, "The root of the problem is poverty. If the Communists in China ease poverty faster than the Indians do, then the Indians will become Communists too. If, on the other hand, China's economy remains stagnant while the economies of its neighbors surge forward, then the Communists will follow the Kuomintang into limbo."

Thanks to men like Nelson Rockefeller and other like-minded leaders, we have already done more in Latin America than in any other part of the world. It is precisely because we have been good neighbors in Latin America that this is the part of the world which is least likely to go Communist. Yet the possibilities in Latin America have hardly been scratched.

Brazil's potential hydroelectric resources exceed those of any other in the world—far, far more than she will need in centuries. The Amazon contains more water than any three other rivers combined, indeed, one-fifth of all the fresh water in the world.

The sick world is in desperate need of our medical knowledge. We can still be of tremendous assistance to the health of Latin America. Malaria, dysentery resulting from bad sanitation and bad water, venereal disease, jungle fever, smallpox, hookworm, and malnutrition are some of the diseases which medical science can reduce or stop.

The tsetse fly is all across the center of Africa. It has been keeping down the population of men and cattle in that area for centuries. Now an injection can protect both men and cattle.

Cholera and smallpox and yellow fever and the plague have been conquered and can be wholly stopped.

Malaria strikes 300 million people a year. Malaria and mosquito control at 20 cents per person can practically wipe out the disease all over the world.

There is a bacillus called BCG which can now immunize children against tuberculosis, the worst killer in the world.

Venereal disease, affecting easily half of Africa and a fourth of Asia, can now be cured by penicillin and other means.

Leprosy, for ages the most dreaded of all diseases, can now be clinically cured by the newest drugs, and it seems to be only a matter of time until this disease will be seen upon earth no more. The Church is reducing leprosy more than all other agencies combined.

This is but the beginning in the realm of health.

But imagine our adopting a policy of improving health for profit only! Here certainly is where the Church must do most of the serving, and do it in the spirit of the Great Physician.

Enormous aid can be given all over the world in combating the diseases and insects which kill citrus fruits, cocoa, indeed, most plants and nearly all domestic animals. This know-how can be disseminated through simple literature and by demonstrations, and stores can be located where the insecticides and fumigants can be purchased.

All this and thousands of other types of service are suggested in Espy's *Bold New Program* and in the eight-volume *Bold New Program* Series put out by Public Affairs Institute.

We far excel Russia in this realm of technical experts and mechanics. Indeed, it is precisely in her lack of technicians that Russia is having her greatest trouble. She needs them all, while we have a super-abundance. Why not fight our war where we have the tremendous advantage with our technicians, going out to win the heart of the world with unselfish competent service?

Russia will stir up the desire of the world—let us fulfil it! It is the thing America believes in, excels in; we need not fear competition in service.

Who can exaggerate what American experience in efficient service could accomplish if we would visualize the situation and then go forth to serve and save the world?

But who will do this? Much of it business will do

as an investment. But the Communists will take the world if we do only what is profitable.

Some of it philanthropy will do, but not one per cent of what must be done.

Government and UN will do much, but not nearly enough. It looks as though neither our Congress nor the other nations will offer an adequate appropriation unless they are driven by fear, and then it will be too late. I *hope* I am mistaken, but this seems to be true as I write.

Who, then, will do the *major part?* It ought to be the Church. Compassionate service for the needy multitude, asking nothing in return, is perfect Christlike Christianity. It is saving men and it is saving the world, which is the true function of the Church of Jesus Christ. The true function of the United Nations and of the United States is to persuade the other nations to reform their extortionate money-lending and oppressive landlordism, while the Church lends an adequate hand to help the hungry masses. Is it not clear that we cannot trust this program *exclusively* to men who will help only where they reap a profit? Three-fourths of it can bring no financial dividends, and that is the most crucial three-fourths.

CHAPTER 13

Wanted, More Landowners

When our technical experts study the causes of hunger and misery, they discover that "cause number one" of dissatisfaction and hunger is the feudal system. Nearly all the countries of the world outside the United States and Canada, and some of Europe, have more people on large feudal estates than live on their own land. These are the people who are hungry, miserable, dissatisfied and ready to follow the Communist conspiracies to violence.

In the Philippines, the Huks are from large estates owned by private landlords and the Church. If there were no great estates there would be no Communist threat in the Philippines. When William Howard Taft was Governor General of the Philippines, he saw that landlordism had been the cause of the constant revolts against Spain, and he started to purchase the big estates and resell them to the tenants. He succeeded in purchasing and reselling *half* of these estates. But, alas, the power of the landlords over the government was great enough to prevent his efforts to divide the other half, and now the Philippine Re-

public is threatened by Communists bred by the oppression and misery of the tenants.

When I was a resident of the Philippines, I wrote
a book about their greatest hero, Dr. José Rizal,
martyred in the Spanish period because he became
the champion of the impoverished tenants of great
estates. Landlords are the curse of the Philippines
even today and the chief source of their political corruption.

The Bell report of 1950 made the landlords of the
Philippines furious but it told the truth. John Collier
comments on that report in *The New York Times* for
October 31, 1950, and says, "Usury, peonage, unpro-
ductive landlordism, administrative corruption, must
be ended."

It is this kind of feudal system, with its grip on the
governments, which is responsible for nine-tenths of
the advances of the Communists around the world.
The Communists overthrew feudalism in Russia,
know how it is hated everywhere, and are on the
march to overthrow it in the rest of the world.

America was shocked in the fall of 1950 at the
abortive rebellion in Puerto Rico and the attempt to
assassinate President Truman. Had people known the
truth they would have wondered that the rebellion
waited so long. The level fertile land of Puerto Rico
is practically all occupied by great sugar, tobacco, and
citrus estates, which make enormous profits. Sugar
made a profit of $100 million in fifteen years. The
wages of the sugar workers average $150 a year.
Governor Theodore Roosevelt, Jr., said in 1929:

"The inland districts, from the outskirts of the cane-ridden valleys to the tops of the mountains seethe with human misery, and it is impossible to pass into or out of any city or town without traversing the fringes of unsightly, maladorous, filthy habitations which surround the more prosperous areas."

In 1948, the government divided 70,000 acres before Governor Tugwell was driven out by the landlords. But the mountains are still crowded with poor people, "undernourished, sickly . . . literal skeletons in the U. S. closet."

This is a difficult subject to handle justly, for all estates are not alike. There are great estates where people are treated far better than their neighbors who own their own land. This is the case with the Firestone plantation in Liberia. It is true of many estates in Hawaii. It *could* be true of all estates. But unfortunately the people who can be trusted with irresponsible power over others are in a very small minority. When men can divide arbitrarily with others they *usually* take all they can take without actually "killing the goose that lays the golden egg." Most of the great estates of the world are oppressive, and many of them are practicing plain modern slavery.

If one had written this a year ago he might have been called a Communist or at least a "pink." But now this fact is recognized by most of the world leaders.

One of the greatest values of the United Nations is the speed with which nations learn from one another by their constant intimate interchange of experience. I think most of the members of the United

Nations now see clearly that parasitical landlords must go. If there is no way to abolish the feudal lords legally they will be abolished via the Communist way, by revolution.

The Communist philosophy may be stated thus: Be realistic; admit that the landlords own the governments and that they will never give up voluntarily. Only well-organized revolution, a new government, violent seizure of the land, and liquidation of the landlords can get results.

The Christian agrees with the Communist that the present system of landownership over much of the world is terrible. The difference is that the Communist advocates revolution and violence, while the Christian advocates legal methods to right the wrongs.

The Christian way would be to throw as much light as possible on oppression by landlords, persuade governments where feudalism exists to reform voluntarily, and to pass laws requiring the landlords to sell their land to the tenants or to the state for resale to the tenants.

This Christian way is not just starry-eyed, wishful thinking. It is beginning to happen in some countries and is being strongly advocated in many other countries. In Northern Ireland, the landlords were compelled by law to sell their estates for a reasonable price, and the land was resold to the tenants. Formerly India was cursed by landlordism and the tenants received an estimated income of $13 a year. Since India became free, the princes and landlords are required by the new government to give up their land, but if they do so voluntarily they are reimbursed in such a way that they will not suffer much loss in standard of living and not much loss in prestige.

The Near East is all astir with the realization that they must do something similar to what India has done or be overthrown by the desperate masses. Let us quote from *The New York Times*, November 27, 1950:

ARAB FORUM SIFTS RURAL CONDITIONS
by Albion Ross

Cairo, Nov. 26. An assembly here of economists and experts from throughout the Arab world, meeting under the auspices of the United Nations to study the condition of 75 per cent of the Arab population that works on the land, has described the situation as disastrous. . . .

The assembly will last for three weeks and will be entirely devoted to the desperate condition of the peasantry and means of changing the situation.

Experts and representatives of various Governments were told that the cultivated land is intensely overcrowded, while, with the exception of Egypt, far less than one-half of the cultivated land is employed and in Egypt less than three-quarters of the cultivable area is used. Concentration of the land in the hands of absentee landlords was sharply attacked. Bitter criticism of the conditions was made by Arabs from various countries. . . .

Prof. Said Himadeh of Lebanon stated: "If constructive action is not taken soon, it may become too late. The rural people are awakening. They are beginning to realize the causes of their misery and their discontent. If their problems are not solved lawfully, the presumption is that sooner or later they will attempt their solution by revolution.". . .

Prof. Himadeh stated that the amount of land per

settled rural individual is less than half an acre in Egypt, in Lebanon about one and one-half acres, in Syria and Jordan about two and one-half and in Iraq four acres.

Speaking of the absentee landowner problem, he said:

"In all Arab countries the density of rural population on the cultivated land is greatly aggravated by the extreme inequality in land ownership. In Egypt more than 3,000,000 out of the 4,000,000 people actively engaged in agriculture own no land or less than one acre each. In Syria about half the land surveyed and settled consists of large estates. In Lebanon, contrary to previous estimates, figures show that less than 200 persons own about half the land surveyed. In northern Iraq the degree of inequality in land ownership is similar to that in Syria, but in southern Iraq practically all land is owned by sheiks or city notables."

The New York Times on November 1, 1950, published an article saying that the government of the United States is pushing such land reform in the United Nations. It said:

U. S. AID TO FARM OWNERSHIP TOLD IN U. N. IN RESPONSE TO POLISH MOVE FOR REFORM STUDY

The United States delegation to the United Nations stole the thunder of the Soviet bloc today and seized on a Polish resolution calling for the study of land reform to present the case for the individually-owned and operated family-sized farm.

Senator John J. Sparkman, Democrat of Alabama, speaking as the son of a tenant farmer who became a farm tenant and then a small owning farmer, told the United Nations General Assembly's Economic and Financial Committee in the course of its debate on land reform, of the great achievements of his country in reducing farm tenancy and increasing the number of individually owned and operated farms.

In fourteen years, tenancy was reduced from 42 to 26 per cent, said Senator Sparkman, a member of the United States delegation. Loans up to $50,000,000 a year under the Bankhead-Jones Farm Tenant Purchase Act gave the impetus to this development, he declared.

"In the United States we believe strongly in farm ownership, individual farm ownership," the United States delegate said. "We believe that the land that a man and his family works and on which they make a living ought to belong to him and to his family.

"It is that objective toward which we have been working the last many years, and it is that same kind of program or a similar program that we envisage may very well be encouraged by this General Assembly and by this committee, and might very well be undertaken in many parts of the world."

Announcing "wholehearted" support of this kind of program, Senator Sparkman asked only for an amendment of the Polish draft "that would particularly provide for helping small farmers, individual farmers to own and operate the land out of which they and their family make a living."

The United States representative described the network of farmer-owned co-operatives with many billion dollars in assets through which the United States farmers controlled the purchase, production and marketing phases of their operations. He told how in half a generation electrified farms had been increased from 10 to 86 per cent.

Mieczyslaw Blausztajn of Poland welcomed the United States statement and defended the "production co-operatives"—that is, collectives—introduced in the country's agriculture as means of achieving a higher level of agricultural production.

This is an extremely interesting account, for it shows Poland and the United States in enthusiastic accord on the question of landownership, although Poland is behind the Iron Curtain.

The truth is that Polish farmers, like the other farmers behind the Iron Curtain, are going to resist to the death any effort to take their land and make it the property of the government, as Marxist socialism requires. They want what President Truman has well called "the American form of landownership," every farmer owning the land he farms.

In Russia, in the European satellites, in China, in Korea, the Communists have for the present abandoned the Socialist plan for land. They frankly say this has to be postponed to the indefinite future.

So the present Communist proposal of land reform differs from our own only in one respect—and it is the difference between war and peace. They advocate revolution, seizure of the land, treating the landlords as criminals, killing them or sending them to Siberia. The American proposal is to pass laws requiring the landlords to sell out their estates to their tenants, or to make some other adjustment that will satisfy the people.

America will not longer allow the Russians to "steal our thunder" by introducing our system of land tenure and calling it "Communism." We believe that we can help our allied governments to see that they must correct this world-wide injustice peacefully, as India did, or face the prospect of being destroyed.

Let nobody imagine that this is going to be easy.

In many parts of the world the landlords have control of the government. Being educated, they can manipulate the laws to their advantage. They force the government to raise taxes until people are driven to sell their land and borrow money. Then they loan the money at 30 per cent per year or more. They own both the tenants and the small landowners, body and soul.

Only the threat of total destruction will persuade these landlords to change their system and surrender their absolute power. The Communists are providing the threat and we will provide the persuasion.

We said at the beginning of this chapter that there are estates which are proving a blessing to their tenants. To break these up into small farms under compulsion would be a backward step. Moreover, there are a great many estates where mass production is far more efficent than individual production. Cotton, bananas, rubber, cocoa, hemp, wheat, tobacco, and fifty other products can be grown more economically by using modern machinery on very large fields. From plowing to harvesting, there is enormous advantage in mass production.

How to accomplish this transfer of absolute control from landlords to some better system without disrupting the efficiency of the estate is a technical question which will require the assistance of trained specialists. Neither landlords nor tenants, as a rule, know any way to do it save by the expulsion of landlords and dividing the land among the tenants. But this method means losing all the advantages of mass cultivation and it loses the experience which many

landlords have in efficient management. Many tenants
have been left *worse off* than they were before when
it was done in the wrong way. There are many possibilities. Here are two that have proven satisfactory:

1. The tenants may be organized into unions and
engage in collective bargaining as unions do in
America.

2. The estate may be converted into a co-operative
enterprise, owned jointly by all employes.

Toyohiko Kagawa believes that co-operatives are
the "Christian answer" to Marxian Socialism and to
Communism. The co-operative is private enterprise,
it is the purest type of democracy, and it possesses all
the advantages of mass production. Kagawa accomplished such miracles for the Japanese through or-
ganizing co-operatives that he is loved all over Japan.
In spite of his weak voice, tremendous crowds go to
hear him speak in Japan, and he has won as many as
ten thousand Japanese to Christ in one month. His
service has spoken far louder than his voice.

There is an impressive list of co-operative achievements in other parts of the world.

Co-operatives have been enormously useful to
farmers in America as every farmer will testify.

Beyond all contradiction, co-operatives saved the
economy of Denmark.

Under Gandhi and since, co-operatives became the
best hope of India. In 1935 there were 100,000 credit
co-operatives to fight the terrible moneylenders.

In Nova Scotia, St. Francis Xavier University, finding terrible illiteracy, poverty, and Communist agita-

tion among coal miners, fishermen, and farmers led
the way to co-operatives, lifted the load of poverty,
helped teach the illiterates, brought about a remarkable co-operation of Catholics and Protestants, and
stopped the Communist agitation in its tracks. Haiti,
Bolivia, Mexico, China, Jamaica, and other countries
have called upon men trained in Nova Scotia to help
them.

Many Catholic and Protestant missionaries trained
in co-operative methods are now helping peoples in
hungry areas to form co-operatives. Many thousands
more need to be sent out to introduce this "Christian
answer." It is not only practical Christianity, but it
is also proving itself to be able to make its way in the
competitive world by sheer merit. It is economically
sound as well as ethically good.

As landlords are persuaded, or compelled by fear
or law, to relinquish their irresponsible domination,
the missionary-minded specialists can be at hand to
advise the wisest steps to be taken, and so can become
the guides and friends of everybody.

These co-operative technicians ought to be men of
great Christian fidelity and conscientiousness. For
changing over to co-operatives is far more than changing a policy. Kagawa shows that when led by Christian men it *can* be shot through with the Christian
spirit of the Golden Rule, whereas if it is not guided
by the Christian spirit it can become another form of
greed.

The management of co-operatives must first of all
be drilled in *integrity*. The co-operative is economic
democracy, and it breaks down exactly where de-

mocracy breaks down, at the point of dishonesty. The co-operative does not demand as much high-pressure salesmanship as a private business, but it does demand in its managers a conscientious faithfulness in every small detail. This is why missionaries with a Christian spirit are the finest organizers of co-operatives around the world.

The tenants need to be taught to read and write and to have an intelligent grasp of the meaning of the co-operative, and they, too, need to be drilled in the need for integrity. For they vote for their managers!

Combine honesty with knowledge, and you have a solid foundation.

Oppressive taxes, usurious moneylenders, and feudal estates must go. We must have 100,000 technically trained men of unimpeachable integrity over the world, to help people help themselves. We must give or loan money when these technicians call for it. That is our program. If that is carried out by government and philanthropy and business and the Church, Communism will gain no more headway in the world than it gained in Nova Scotia.

Foreign missionaries stand between callous, rich landlords with governments in their grip on the one hand, and, on the other hand, an utterly unscrupulous gang of Communist thieves and liars who seek to overthrow the landlords and governments in order to make the world one vast prison pen of peons under Moscow. And heedless of the tragedy, the Church in America has left its missionaries with but meager re-enforcements and resources. She did not know her own army. Her sin has found her out.

That diagnosis alone does no good. What shall we do to stop our defeat?

Admit our sin? Not enough.

Back corruption? That is sure defeat; God is against corruption.

Hide the facts? Defeat.

Let Russia have the world by default, while she uses lies and hate and murder? That is to abandon Christ.

Spend $1.26 a year per capita on foreign missions? This way lies defeat.

Be the Good Samaritan of the world honestly, all out, asking no special privileges, every Christian helping adequately—Victory!

"But," one man replied, "we aren't good enough to do that."

My answer was, "Then we'd better get that good, and fast!"

CHAPTER 14

How the Church Can Help

It is the Church, more than any other organization public or private, that ought to see the Technical Assistance program of Point IV through to a marvelous success.

What we need is an adequate plan of campaign. In a military campaign everything is worked out for everybody to the smallest detail. This is what we need now for the Church and for each Church member. We shall make a beginning in this chapter.

A Committee on Technical Co-operation has been appointed by the Division of Foreign Missions of the National Council of Churches to aid Point IV. This committee ought to be increased to a wide representation of the most influential and dynamic Christians in America. It ought to have an adequate staff and an ample budget. Then it should become the Church's arm of the great agencies of U.S. and U.N. which are building up a reserve bank of available technical experts.

This Committee on Technical Co-operation would reach in two directions, inward and outward:

1. *In* toward the churches.
2. *Out* toward the main agencies ready to help that world.

1. REACHING INTO THE CHURCHES

Let us first describe how the Committee on Technical Co-operation might seek in the churches the type of technicians needed throughout the world.

It could, in co-operation with the denominational boards, contact ministers of churches where technical men might be found. I do not think it would be wise at first to send a letter to all the ministers in the United States. I should think a pilot trial might be made with certain selected ministers. These ministers might talk with men and women in their congregations who possess technical skills and Christian character and let them read this book to help give them the vision of saving the world, and ask that they permit their names to be placed in the "reserve bank" of technicians who may later be needed.

This reserve bank of names could include those of men of experience, some of them perhaps ready to retire, some of them able to pay a part of their expenses. The experience of many men and women over sixty years of age would be priceless.

This inquiry would be made without any publicity. The congregation would not know anything about the project until the technicians in their church were actually called into service.

This first pilot project, with ten ministers, would guide the committee as it reached out to a larger

number of churches. For the second pilot experiment
I would suggest that one hundred ministers be selected. They would be told that they were chosen because their judgment was trusted in helping find the
best way to discover technically trained men and
women of vision and Christian character. They would
be asked to get into touch with men and women in
their congregations who might make valuable contributions abroad and request that they permit their
names to be placed on the reserve list.

The third pilot or trial project might be with a
thousand ministers. I should think that by that time
the Committee would know how to approach all the
other churches. It is such a new field that these pilot
experiments should guide the Committee. But they
should not be dragged out over many months, for
time is running out.

2. Reaching out to the World

Meanwhile the Committee on Technical Co-operation would get into touch with organizations which
need technicians for world service, so that it could be
a bridge from the supply to the demand.

Organizations which require technicians overseas
are of three general classes:

A. Official
   The United States
   The United Nations and its specialized agencies
   Nations seeking technical assistance

B. Industry and Business
   Firms of every kind doing international business

C. Philanthropy and Religion

All mission boards, including YMCA and YWCA

Foundations doing overseas service

CARE, Near East Relief, and other relief agencies

Schools and colleges operating in the Near East and elsewhere

American colleges with outreach abroad, as "Yale in China"

Service clubs, like Rotary, serving abroad

Women's clubs

Our Committee could, I think, do much more than ask these organizations what technicians they require. It could *stimulate* them to *see the vision* of saving the world by sharing our know-how. It could suggest the need of selecting new personnel so that they would influence the character and ideals of a country as well as its business interests.

The committee could keep insisting that the purpose of Point IV is to save the world from dangerous despair, and not to exploit need for profit.

This committee could also influence churches to do their part through missions in saving the world from disaster. Missions did not start with that purpose. Tho vast majority of Christians do not realize that they have any responsibility or power to save the peace through missions.

PROPOSAL TO CONDUCT A QUICK SURVEY

The Student Volunteer Movement publishes an annual bulletin called "Christian Horizons"; it tells what types of missionaries the various Mission Boards are seeking. No church publication as yet describes what kinds of technicians the retarded areas of the world *need* and *want,* though such studies have been made for some countries.

If we ask *only* government officials at the top to tell us, we shall get a lopsided and inadequate answer. They will look at the country from the viewpoint of politicians and of the ruling classes rather than from the viewpoint of the people in misery. Any American can understand how inadequate would be a reply as to the needs of America solely from a political viewpoint. What, for example, would it say about religion or racial relations?

The Committee on Technical Co-operation could conduct a supplemental survey of its own at small cost to add to the knowledge it could gain from other surveys. Nearly every country has one or more missionaries who are also true diplomats, with rich contacts with officials and leaders in all walks of life. Indeed, the American public would be astonished and thrilled if it realized what a tremendous influence these missionary ambassadors wield in Latin America, in Asia, and in Africa. Here is one suggestion for using these missionary diplomats to help with our survey.

Suppose we asked an experienced missionary statesman, one who is famous throughout all that land, to represent us in India. He might secure a copy of the *Dictionary of Technical Skills* published by the Department of Labor of the United States Government, he might carry this book with him as he visited the recognized leaders of industry and of all professions in India. He might say:

"I thought you might be interested in this dictionary of the technological skills of the United States. The American people are eager to exchange technological knowledge with you. If you will kindly accept this book as a present, I should be glad to have you mark in it what skills you feel India could give to the U.S.A. and what America in turn could give to India. If we find men and women of the highest type of character, with a great love of their fellow men, who love India and desire to be helpful, it is possible that we may later send them here at the invitation of your government. This is a preliminary inquiry only. It is made with an earnest desire to draw our countries closer together in mutual co-operation."

If this kind of approach were made in India to, say, a hundred men high in the professions and in industry, the results ought to be illuminating. If similar inquiries were going on in other countries the total findings ought to be important enough to be published and furnished to all mission boards.

Many boards have been seeking only such types of missionaries as the missionaries already on the field report they need. This is not an adequate guide, because a non-technical missionary is not competent to see the technical needs, just as an untrained man could not recognize mineral-bearing rocks, or the need for better fertilizer. Surveying needs and wants is in itself an expert task.

This Committee on Technical Co-operation could be one of the most effective committees in America if it had adequate resources. Composed of highly skilled men, it might develop into the most useful agency in the world in saving men from desperate violence. It could be of enormous assistance to the United Nations, to the United States, to all international business enterprises, to philanthropies and churches. It ought to be non-sectarian, so that it could serve Roman Catholics, Protestants, and Jews alike.

The entire "Bold New Program" is stupendous in its possibilities, beyond anything ever contemplated before. It is beyond the purpose of this book to indicate what vast doors of opportunity are open for government, for the United States, for business, for philanthropy. We cannot undertake here to outline even what missions could do. That would in itself require several volumes. When Overseas Consultants surveyed the needs of Iran, its findings filled six large volumes. The moment one begins to examine what missions could do in any country, we see many volumes to be written!

Where would the Church get the money with which to meet the opportunities which this world presents for Christian service for human need?

By training people to tithe. They are now being compelled to give thirty per cent of their income; those in the high brackets of income must pay the government fifty, sixty, seventy, eighty per cent of their incomes. But fifteen per cent of their income is exempt from taxation if they give it for religious and philanthropic objects. People should be taught to give five per cent of their income for the local and national church, including home missions; five per cent for the foreign missions program, and the remaining exempted five per cent for other philanthropy, like the community chest.

Neither home missions nor churches nor community chests would suffer, because five per cent is more than people are now giving for either. The amount for foreign missions, if all of the forty million Protestants gave their five per cent, would be around two billion dollars a year. The average income of Protestants is a good deal above the estimated income for all adults, over $1,000 per year. Five per cent of their incomes would be more than $50. Forty millions at $50 each would be two billion dollars. That would be ample to place a hundred thousand technically trained missionaries in the field and give them $20,000 each to spend.

All the Protestant churches together are giving an average of $1.26 per member for their foreign missionaries, less than two and a half cents a week! They are compelled to give an average of more than $20 a week for *hot war*, and they *voluntarily* give two and a half cents a week to win the *cold war*. That is because they are utterly ignorant of the fact that missionaries are their soldiers in the cold war which we are rapidly losing. If they knew, they would give. Americans are generous.

Fifty thousand or a hundred thousand of the type of Christian technicians that one can find in the Christian churches would quickly change the attitude of the hungry three-fourths of mankind.

It is not necessary for the projects to be *finished*, or even half finished. The very initiation of this program would send an electric thrill over all the world.

People would see their best hope to be good will, co-operation, education—not violence.

This and this alone is the way to help the Russians to see that the Christian way is the best. If the multitudes turned away from hate and violence and began to follow the way of peace and love and education and co-operation, the men in Moscow would see that the Christian way works better than their own. So long as their way succeeds, they will never abandon it.

Stalin and the other members of the Russian Communist Party have never had an opportunity to see real Christianity in action. In the Czarist regime they saw the unspeakable Rasputin, who had such influence in high places, and they loathed the type of false Christianity he embodied. How will they ever see Jesus unless they see Jesus in us? If they saw Him incarnated in a compassionate and humble America the Russian leaders would love that Christ! If Rasputin and his kind had not betrayed Christian Russia there would today be no peril of atheistic totalitarianism sweeping the rest of the non-Christian world under the Iron Curtain. Rasputin betrayed Christ by his collusion with the Czarist oppression; we have betrayed Christ by indifference.

It is very, very late now, but not too late.

There are many reasons why the Church should assume a leading part in this program.

First, it *is* Christianity. Much so called Christianity is only Christianity upward, not outward, because it *omits* compassionate service for the neediest of all people.

Second, this is the way to win the remainder of the world to Christ.

Third, the Church has the *kind* of men and women who ought to go out and help the world.

Fourth, America believes in free enterprise doing all it can do, with help from government only where necessary. The Christian Church is free enterprise, and its business is to help the world.

Fifth, we cannot leave the lifting of the world only to capital, for capital invests only where it gets a profit. The only profit the Church seeks is saved souls.

Sixth, Christians need this service for their own souls' salvation. The Church languishes for want of a burning cause. The youth of the Church need a crusade to which they can dedicate their lives with devoted abandon. This is the crusade! The older people need a cause to which to give their money and their ardent prayers. When we begin to burn to lift the miserable two-thirds of the world out of its misery and despair, we shall ourselves have a Pentecost.

Seventh, millions of people want to try Christianity in all-out world action. Millions who feel ugly and more or less un-Christian in being compelled to spend a third to a half of their income in building bombs and planes, which they hope will never be used, need an alternative in which they can invest in construction instead of in destruction, in love instead of in fear, in peace-making instead of war-making. Most of the Christian Church is ripe for this bold Christian program.

Chapter 15

It Must Be Christian Character

The technicians we send abroad must be more than technicians. They must have the quality of personality which the Church at its best produces. They must have warm hearts, democratic freedom from snobbery (which diplomats often lack), a great love of their fellow men, total color blindness so that they will reveal not the slightest awareness of racial prejudice, a Christlike longing to help. They must have integrity and frank honest character, they must be lovable because they love everybody, seeing the best in people and knowing how to show them appreciation. They must not only help people but also win their love. They must have the spirit of the missionary at his best, who works among the masses because he passionately longs to serve men and to help his world, and not because he is getting a fat salary.

Where are such men and women? They are in the churches. I have come to believe that they are in American churches by the hundreds of thousands. This is why the Christian Church ought to assume the major rôle for finding and supplying men and women to lift the world out of its misery.

For these men and women we are sending abroad
are just as useful in educating the characters and
ideals of people as in giving the technical knowledge.

A man whose mind is educated and whose heart is
evil is a menace. Education enables a man of bad will
to do more harm. Robert Millikan, Nobel Prize win-
ner and great Christian, calls Nouy's *Human Des-
tiny* "the greatest book of a century." That book says:
"The conflict between pure intelligence and moral
values has become a matter of life and death. Intelligence alone, not subjected to moral values, has led
to monstrosities." All knowledge is dangerous when
the heart is wrong.

Who has heard one of the Russian representatives
speak over the radio without marveling at his brilliant
mind and at the same time being pained by listening
to his perfectly immoral distortion of truth and his
intentional lies? That type of utter disregard of integrity in an intelligent man like him is the most
dangerous thing this world could have.

This is the reason why it would be magnificent if
the education of illiterates could be achieved by
Christian churches and missions. The general average
of character would be higher than when the education
is purely secular. A literacy campaign is like a school
in this respect; its quality is determined very largely
by the character of the men and women at the top.
This is also the reason why all the technicians whom
we send abroad should have sterling Christian honor.
If they have honest integrity they will spread integrity among all those who are working with them.

We are trying to persuade the world to adopt democracy, yet most democracies tend to break down and become democracies only in name. In every case one cause of this failure is a lack of integrity. Lack of honesty is working more havoc than lack of knowledge.

Democracy is the best government in the world, but it demands a high general level of character among the masses. It is only as good as the general average, for it is government by the majority. The people tend to select their kind for office.

If the average man is willing to sell out his vote to the highest bidder, then the man who buys his vote does not represent honesty but crooked politics. Where votes can be bought, the election goes to the man who can spend the most to buy them. Corruption breeds corruption.

After such a man is elected he at once lays plans to get his investment back, and to the extent that other men in his government were elected on the same dishonest basis he can conspire with them to alter the law so that they can legally drain off the revenues of the country into their own pockets. Only an idiot breaks laws! The smart crook changes the laws so that he will not need to violate them.

There are "democracies" in which all elected officials became millionaires in one term of office, while nominally receiving very modest salaries.

When government becomes too oppressive, more and more victims conspire against it or rise in open rebellion, only to be liquidated by the police. Then the army must be strengthened to suppress violence and laws must be made to punish patriots and to reward corruption.

At last, oppressive and corrupt governments have trouble with the very armies which they create to defend themselves. Some military leader, no more honest than the politicians, sees his opportunity and as a pseudo champion of the rights of the oppressed people rides to the capital at the head of his army and chases out or kills or imprisons the government officials. The republic becomes a military dictatorship, a fascist government. It is then just as totalitarian as the so-called "republics" of the Soviet Union.

This tragic and very common deterioration of democracy stems back, in the first place, to the corruptibility of the average voter. If he had not been willing to sell out his country for a few pieces of silver or for some personal advantage, he would have voted for the best men available, and government would have remained clean.

Every country has a perpetual fight between the forces of corruption and the forces of good government. We have such a struggle in America just because we have good and bad, selfish and public-spirited citizens. In many countries the balance between good and bad is so nearly equal that the personal influence and example of a few men in high position determine whether these countries will remain truly free or deteriorate into dictatorships.

Suppose we placed a hundred thousand Americans of unimpeachable integrity all over the world, setting countries an example of straight, open, honest American honor at its best. They would have more influence for world righteousness than all the money America possesses. They would tip the scales.

American leaders know that the billions they have loaned to other countries have been used unwisely or stolen so frequently that often little or none of the money has reached down to the people for whom it was intended. We are a generous nation, but we are determined no longer to be "suckers." Perhaps one reason that foreign missions have received less enthusiastic support than formerly is that we have been so disappointed in the results of our enormous loans. This is unjust to missions, for nobody has ever accused missions of misusing or stealing money— they never have enough! But the countries where the missionaries work have often lost our money, and the missionary cause has suffered as a consequence.

UNRRA is one of the programs which disappointed us in this respect. We know that a large proportion of the goods we gave through that agency found its way to black markets. A young man in the Philippines told me, "We thought UNRRA would heal our wounds, but, instead, it has broken our hearts." Americans on the inside now see that if UNRRA had called upon missionaries to administer their funds and merchandise, very little of it would ever have reached the black market. By and large, missionaries are the most honest people in the world, and unquestionably they know the needy people as no other foreigners can know them.

We ought never to loan or give money or charity of any kind to a country until we have conscientious men and women with a missionary spirit, who speak the language of the country, who have exact knowledge of the situation, and who are capable of seeing that the money is not misused or misappropriated.

There is no reason why America should ever again be deceived as so often we have been deceived in the past. There is every reason why we should not. It is bad for a country to be allowed to misuse millions or billions.

The Church has the stupendous and even terrifying responsibility to produce men with conscience, passion to serve, sterling integrity, and true technical skill, and it must see that such men are used all over the world. The Church must lift not only the minds of men, but also their souls, their integrity, their love.

Chapter 16

Prayer for the United Nations

While Christians join in reaching down to help
the hungry two-thirds at the bottom of society, they
must also reach up to pray for the men who are struggling to find the pathway to peace through the United
Nations. Christians can be far more influential by
praying for the members of the United Nations than
they dream.

Indeed, a few thousand praying Christians *are*
wielding far greater influence right now than other
people believe is the case. The Laymen's Movement
for a Christian World, made up of Christian business
and professional men, began five years ago to pray
for the United Nations. They send men to attend
daily sessions of the Security Council and the Assembly and pray in silence. The Laymen's Movement has printed and distributed upon request over
a million cards bearing the names of the delegates
and asking people to pray for them, and write them
letters.

These men have become acquainted with many of
the delegates, and have their confidence. Largely

through their influence the Fifth General Assembly of the United Nations opened September 19, 1950, with one minute of silent prayer. Here is a description of it:

When the vote was taken in the General Assembly in October of 1949 to place a moment of silent prayer on the agenda, not one vote was cast against it.

Ambassador Warren R. Austin, speaking in New York on Sunday evening, Sept. 17, 1949, said: "At three o'clock on Tuesday, September 19th, the delegations of the fifty-nine nations of the United Nations will convene for the opening of the most crucial General Assembly since San Francisco. Before they begin to tackle the vital issues of peace, they will observe a minute of silence for individual prayer or meditation.

"At that moment I hope the people of America will pause in their homes, their shops, on their farms, and in the streets, wherever they may be, to offer up their prayers for God's blessing upon the United Nations, and for a peace with liberty and justice for all men."

In continuing his remarks, Ambassador Austin said: "The Laymen's Movement has long worked for such reliance on prayer. This is a welcome suggestion."

Five members of the Laymen's Movement were present at the opening session and were moved by the reverent manner in which General Carlos P. Romulo, the retiring president, introduced this new procedure. General Romulo said: "This Assembly, often described in the past as a mere international debating society, has the chance to grow into a virtual Parliament of Man. It has the chance to save the United Nations and the peace of the world.

"Let us pray to Almighty God to grant us the vision and the courage to discharge this awesome responsibility. I invite the representatives to rise and observe one minute of silence dedicated to prayer or meditation."

The hearts of many people were raised in prayer all across the country at the same hour. (Laymen's Movement for a Christian World.)

When a photograph taken during the moment of silent prayer in the United Nations was sent to Ambassador Austin by the Laymen's Movement, Mr. Austin responded with the following letter:

UNITED STATES REPRESENTATIVE
TO THE UNITED NATIONS

New York 16, New York
October 28, 1950

Dear Wallace Speers and Weyman Huckabee:

You have made very real to me the love and omnipotence of our Heavenly Father through your personal conversations with me and your letters.

I am delighted to have the photograph of the General Assembly in that moment of prayer with which it opened the present Session. This was an historic event, great enough to make such a souvenir especially precious. But you have added to its meaning by your lovely inscription.

Thanking you with a full heart, I am,

Sincerely yours,

WARREN R. AUSTIN

Mr. Wallace C. Speers, Chairman
Mr. Weyman C. Huckabee, Secretary
The Laymen's Movement for a
    Christian World, Inc.
347 Madison Avenue
New York 17, New York

Warren Austin has many times thanked the Laymen's Movement for praying for him. He said he had come to rely on them more than upon any other human source to help him to keep his mind free from prejudice and hate so as to see every issue dispassionately and with a clear mind.

What the Laymen's Movement suggests, and what Warren Austin approves, is for all of us Christians everywhere to pray for the delegates, and to write one letter a day or a week to different delegates, in turn, saying that we are praying for them in their tremendous responsibility—that they may receive God's wisdom and so bring peace on earth, and good will among men. Thus in the course of a few months each delegate will get a great many letters. Mr. Austin said he gets thousands of letters from people who are praying for him, and that he tries to answer every letter, because he values them so highly. We can help the delegates win the peace if we pray for and write to all the men in the General Assembly of the United Nations.

The Prayer Call card, *Standing in the Need of Prayer* (5¢ each), with the names of all delegates, may be obtained from the Laymen's Movement, 347 Madison Avenue, New York City, upon request.

By joining in this ever widening prayer army you help produce the spiritual atmosphere in which, if anywhere, men can agree upon the pathway to a just and lasting peace.

If each of these men got a *million* letters from people, never criticizing but only assuring them they are being held up with prayer, *that* would give them a new confidence in the heart of America, and a new sense of the power of God.

We are not weak when we raise our voices in prayer for all government officials and reach down through our missionaries and laymen to the pathetic hungry people at the bottom as they hold up their hands, asking, "Who will help us?" We are not weak when we thus combine prayer and loving service. If we should follow this practice we would become the most powerful people in the world, for we would be *channels* for the limitless power of God's spirit, and demonstrate that right is might.

You and I have been looking everywhere for the answer. *We* are the answer, if we help the masses and pray for the leaders. We have been God's *problem* because we in America have failed to see and do these two things *adequately.* Let us all stop being God's problem and become His answer. Wringing our hands in helpless desperation is not only weak, it is also wicked. Stop it, oh, ye of little faith, and pray and write and help need. Be strong. "We have hard work to do and loads to lift."

There are Christians in the United States who strongly emphasize repentance, and who will say that this book has not done enough in merely confessing our sins and repenting them. For example, why have we not shown how, historically, the oppression and insolence of the white race has built up a tremendous tide of resentment throughout the non-white world? Is it because we did not realize this? No; I realize it. But I think that the Communists have overdone confessing for us, and certainly they have distorted the truth. Moreover, post-mortems do little good, especially when they stir up grievances which we hope good deeds will help people to forget. We need good deeds, not repining.

And as for repenting, there are two kinds. Judas repented and committed suicide. It would be easier for us to say our prayers and "repent" and continue the way we have been going until our folly results in the death of hope than to repent in *deed* and not in word only. It costs less to coast along—while the coasting lasts. The word "repent" originally meant "turn around and go the other way." From cover to cover, this book says "turn around, Christians of America, and go the other way."

It has but one purpose. That is to point out what a marvelous opportunity we have to win the friendship of the world through unselfishly serving it, and to inspire the Christian Church with new courage and fresh vision.

The other ways have failed. Try Christ's way. We who have tried it are thrilled at its magic!

POSTSCRIPT:

Lift the World or Lose It!

Wake Up or Blow Up was published in March, 1951. In it I outlined a way of saving from Communism the lands still outside of the Iron Curtain by a program of service joined in by business and missions and the technical agencies of the United States and the United Nations.

It is now September, 1951. I have spent six of these eight months traveling around the fringes of the Iron Curtain—in South Asia, North Africa, and the Middle East.

Everything I have found there convinces me of the soundness of the program offered in this book.

Our literacy teams visited the tragic camps, where 850,000 Arab refugees broke our hearts with their gratitude. In the camp at Bethlehem, a thousand thronged around us, speaking frantically in a language we could not understand. But we understood these tearful, pleading eyes! Theirs was the heart-rending appeal of the disinherited three-fifths of the human race—illiterate, and defenseless because they are illiterate!

We met other Arabs in Syria and Iraq, where, in the Tigris and Euphrates Valleys, the United Nations has an enormous irrigation project in the planning stage. But it will be five years before these UN ditches are dug—and meanwhile the seething camps of hungry, desperate Arabs are breeding Communists by the thousand.

We found just such Communist breeding-grounds in every country in South Asia, except Afghanistan. The peoples of Southern Asia are dangerously unhappy, vascillating excitedly between our ideals and those of Russia. On this continent live half the human race, all of them tormented by fear and uncertainty, the hot center of the world's cold war; here is China, gone behind the Iron Curtain; here is India, fighting against it and favoring democracy; here thousands of Communist agents sow the seeds of hatred of the West, hatred of all Americans, hatred of all who own anything, and promises of Utopia when these "enemies of the people" have been destroyed.

Against the Communist agents stand the United Nations and the United States, fighting with the weapon of friendly assistance—with deeds of mercy against poisonous words. It is a tremendously powerful and effective weapon, and the Russians fear it, deeply.

Isador Lubin, the American representative to the UN, told that body that Russia had not contributed "one red ruble to international efforts for the relief and betterment of undeveloped regions" (*New York Times*, August 8, 1951). The delegate from Communist Russia immediately flew into a rage and bitterly attacked all UN relief programs. Russia hates Western relief and with good reason!

Or consider Iran, another Asian danger spot. A huge plague of locusts this year threatened to destroy the food crops of Iran, which would have meant a famine. American airplanes came, sprayed poison on the locusts and destroyed them (at a trifling cost), saved the crops, and won the deep gratitude of the Iranians. I heard that slaughter of the locusts discussed all over Asia. It created the goodwill necessary to get Conciliator Averill Harriman into Iran, in the midst of the Iran-Britain oil dispute. Our kindness to Iran in her hour of peril conditioned her to listen to us when she would listen to no one else. Loving kindness is not only Christian; it is the most powerful weapon in the world.

In Afghanistan, a country never conquered by a foreign power or exploited by foreign business, we saw ten thousand hungry, landless nomads (their fathers have been landless since the dawn of history) going out to settle on their own land and cultivate fields irrigated by Morrison and Knutson, an American firm. Such companies, working for Asian governments, are helping to save that continent from revolution and despair—and from Communism!

It isn't all smooth sailing yet, thanks to greedy native landlords who would keep the natives down as enslaved share-croppers, and the Communist propagandists, who describe Western aid as a Western imperialist plot. India, Pakistan, Indonesia, and Indo-China are still smarting under the wounds of that old imperialism, and Communist propaganda is so effective that Western financial aid has been rejected in many instances, even when it was desperately needed.

But the most dangerous enemy of technical and financial assistance is not the propaganda of Russia; it is the continuing ignorance of the American people! Because they do not yet see that this service of loving kindness is the only weapon that can save Asia, men in Congress, and too many American business men, in an effort to reduce taxes, would cut this service to the bone, while they increase our appropriations for war! They do not yet understand that the real war for survival is being fought in Asia by our technical experts.

I agree with Justice Douglas (in *Look Magazine*, August, 1951) that the course India and the countries around her will take is far more important than whether we are to stop fighting on or beyond the 38th parallel in Korea. Douglas says that we are so obsessed with the military viewpoint that we have no other viewpoint, and he is right. Generals have led us through two world wars, and their influence is enormous. We trust them to save Asia. But, you see, generals are West Point men, trained to think in terms of war and armaments, and not that wars of poisonous propaganda must be fought with unselfish service. And America, following the generals, closes its ears to the fatal truth that we *cannot* save Asia by a display of military might.

General Eisenhower tells us that our superiority is so great that we need not fear the Russians. That is good news. But Russian propaganda is far more effective than Russian arms, and you cannot kill that with a bomb or a gun. Unless we use the right weapons now, Russia can, and probably will, capture Asia and Africa without firing a shot. Russia has not yet lost a man in Korea!

Governor Dewey found not one war but five wars in Asia, all Communist-inspired. I found five revolutions going on at the same time in Burma, all inspired by Russia. Douglas says we are losing Asia. We have not lost Asia yet but we shall lose it, unless we stop the present drift to Communism by going all-out to help Asia the peaceful way.

This service program is a big program—so stupendous that it cannot be accomplished by the UN or the United States alone, or by any private philanthropy, or by any one church. It must be a world-wide effort on the part of all men who love truth and freedom.

We shall *not* beat Communist propaganda with the Voice of America alone, or with any other propaganda alone. We must add works to words. Norman Cousins was in India while Congress was debating whether or not to send two million tons of wheat to India. I was there, too; I read every derogatory word leveled by our "statesmen" at India; I read it in Indian *Communist* publications. I agreed with Cousins when he wrote back to America: "If Congress doesn't want to give wheat—let us recall the appropriation for the Voice of America. Let us shut down our efforts to combat Communist propaganda. . . . There is no point in our telling our story if we have no story to tell."

Exactly! If we don't want to meet the terrible longing and need of the peoples of Asia, we have no story to tell. And the more we boast, the more they will hate us!

Thank God, the common (Christian) people of America forced Congress to act! Driven by personal convictions of isolationism and economy, suspicion, dislike of Nehru's policies, or partisan opposition of everything President Truman proposes, Congress pottered and squirmed and argued about wheat for India for a solid year. The Indian people watched their neighbors die of starvation while Congress dawdled, and they thought it an incredible display of callous indifference, racial prejudice and greed. When Congress finally acted and the wheat began to flow into India, there was a profound reaction in India. Madame Pandit, the Indian Ambassador to the United States, lost her heart to the American people. Nehru wrote: "This generous gesture . . . will evoke a friendly response in India, and bring the two peoples nearer together." India was saved from Communism, at least for another year!

This experience in India ought to teach us what Christian America and the Christian Church in America can do! We can stop the burning crusade of Communist hatred if and when we become aflame once more with the gospel of love which swept the earth in the early centuries.

Here is another fact that you may read with amazement: Christian missionaries may still enter nearly every non-Christian country to serve their needs, even when the UN and the United States are held off in suspicion and where foreign corporations are suspect. Sixty countries have asked the World Literacy Committee to help them, even though some of those countries have refused the aid of the U.S. Government. They know we will *not* forge new chains of imperialism. The Indonesian government, having just driven out the Dutch and still suspicious of all Western gestures, has just invited us to help them.

Some of the missionaries in Communist China have been asked to remain and work at the expense of the Communist Government, in spite of our war with China. Many will return to Korea when the war ends there. It is true that in some countries missionaries are prevented from proselytizing, but in *every* country their aid is sought in health, sanitation, agriculture, home economics, nutrition, and child care.

The Church *alone* cannot save the world in the present crisis. It will require the assistance of many agencies, public and private. But, on the other hand, all our efforts will fall flat unless the Church discovers and sends forth an army of technically skilled men and women with the flaming love and the glorious integrity of Christ. Our technical skills must be matched by a higher type of integrity and love and character than the world now has. We are not safe with more power until we have more character. It is that Christian character that the Church can and must contribute in the technicians we send abroad.

Your part now is to tell everybody, everywhere, every day, of this desperate need and this imperative crusade for Christ and humanity. Your part now is to add your fuel to this spreading Christian fire, to make it a fire more consuming than Communist treachery and deceit, hotter and a lot more creative than the fire of the hydrogen bomb. Either we do that, or the Communists win!